# Trust and Obey

## A Story of God's Faithfulness

By
Michael Youssef, Ph.D.

# Contents

## Trust and Obey: A Life Motto

When I was a boy of 12, I used to hear my older brother, Nathan, singing in English. His favorite song was "Trust and Obey." I had limited facilities in English, so I thought he was saying, "Yesterday." I never asked him, but I often wondered why he was singing about the past.

Even as a young boy I was future-oriented. I always had future dreams. I dreamed of getting away from home, being independent, and making money like my banker brothers. Those daydreams often intensified when I experienced failure or perceived unjust punishment from my father.

Actually, I dreamed of doing better than my brothers. But I was the runt of the family. My accomplished siblings were as much as 19 years older than me, and my parents seemed to believe there was no way I could equal their success, let alone exceed it.

Thus, I could not understand why my brother would sing about yesterday. Surely he should sing a song that said, "Tomorrow . . . tomorrow." At least, that was my secret song. Tomorrow, I will leave home. Tomorrow, I will experience freedom from parental control, oppressive culture, and severe societal limitation.

Although God had graciously planted that desire in my heart, the freedom He ultimately had in mind was quite different. It would not entail just political and societal freedom, but more importantly, the spiritual freedom that Jesus gave me. Later I understood that spiritual freedom was far higher, far greater, and far more lasting than simply escaping my oppressive environment. It would take years before I understood what Nathan was singing.

It was not "Yesterday"; it was "Trust and Obey." That not only became a meaningful song, but it would represent my entire life's journey.

You may be asking, "What's all that got to do with the history of The Church of The Apostles?" It has everything to do with it. "Trust and obey" became the map to be followed—not just for me, but for the first 25-year history of the church.

When I am invited to speak to pastors and others about the growth of The Church of The Apostles, I tell them, "Save yourself the trouble." We did not establish our church by following a 20-step strategy or by breaking down 25 goals into 5-year plans. If I were to give a speech on the growth of our church, it would be the shortest speech I have ever given. I would simply say, "Trust and obey," and then I would sit down.

Why then am I writing a book to explain what those two words represent? Very simply, to document the inner workings of that statement during a 25-year period. What happened when we did trust and obey, and what were the consequences when we did not?

This is a book about God's faithfulness. His faithfulness to me as an individual when I was hopelessly unfaithful, and His faithfulness to me as the struggling founding pastor of a marvelous vineyard of His own planting. But above all, this is a book about His faithfulness to His word and His promises, both of which The Church of The Apostles relies upon to this day.

*Michael*

Michael Youssef, Ph.D.
Atlanta, Georgia
February 2012

*Chapter One*

## From My Beginnings

While I was growing up in Egypt, I often heard the story. But I will never forget the first time I heard the entire account.

Our family was a member of a Christian minority. My maternal grandfather was a pillar in the Plymouth Brethren Movement. My paternal grandfather was a nominal Coptic Orthodox, but my father was an elder in the Free Methodist church that we attended.

As far back as I can remember I felt a deep affection for our pastor, Ayad Girgis. He was a grandfatherly type who showed me genuine affection. He baptized me when I was four years old. When I was still fairly young, he moved to another town, and his departure saddened me. Yet he returned to our hometown annually for our denomination's synod assembly. Whenever he came, I was the one who insisted that he stay in our home.

One day, two of my older brothers were joking with me about my special feelings for Pastor Girgis and the relationship we shared. One of them finally said, "After all, it's understandable, isn't it? If it had not been for him, Michael, you wouldn't be alive today."

"Really? What do you mean?" I asked. "How did he save my life?"

Both of them were surprised that I didn't know about Pastor Girgis's involvement. So my brother Nader told me the details.

***

The story began in February 1948. By then, my parents already had six children, the oldest being 18. Then a terrible shock came. My mother, Noza, realized she was expecting a seventh child. The news of another child devastated my mother because her health was already deteriorating and she suffered from a mild form of rheumatism that was growing more painful. "I can't raise another child," she said. "Physically, I cannot go through that again."

"Yes, this is too much," said Amerhome, my father. "Your health won't permit another pregnancy."

They immediately called the doctor and asked his advice. He said quite frankly, "You must have an abortion because the pregnancy threatens your health."

My father agreed. The doctor scheduled my mother to go in for an abortion two days later.

In our community, abortion was not uncommon. Although my parents were Christians, they were impacted by the Islamic culture that does not value human life like Christianity does.

We lived in a city that had a decent medical facility. My hometown of Assiut, more than 250 miles from Cairo, had been a haven for Christians for more than 1,400 years. Presbyterians, Assemblies of God, and Methodists had built their mission headquarters there, but the Presbyterians had established a large, first-class hospital as well.

The decision to abort was settled that evening as my father visited their pastor and told him the situation.

"Yes, yes, I understand," said Pastor Girgis. "It seems the sensible thing to do." He promised to pray for my parents as they

8

went through this ordeal. As the two men parted, Pastor Girgis said, "But, Amerhome, you know, we must be careful not to tamper with the will of God."

My father understood that as a warning. But the will of God seemed clear. Another baby could gravely affect my mother's health.

Consequently, my parents planned to move ahead with the abortion.

It was early enough in her pregnancy that it involved little risk, and yet, she couldn't get her mind off what was going to take place. She wasn't worried, only disturbed, as if some gnawing thought tried to reach her consciousness. *Why do I feel disturbed about this?* she wondered. *After all, it is the sensible thing to do considering my medical problem.*

Then, that same night, after the evening church service, Pastor Girgis talked with my parents again. "I understand the consequences of what I am telling you," he said. "But you must trust God and go through with this pregnancy. I am well aware of your health problem. But I sense that this one will serve God's purpose. I would not have told you this, if I did not believe it."

My poor mother hardly knew what to say. For days she had not been feeling well, and this was not what she wanted to hear. She stared at my father, who looked startled by the message.

"God is involved in this pregnancy, Noza," the pastor said. "He will give you the necessary health and the strength to cope with another child."

Nevertheless, my parents hesitated, more out of confusion than anything else. "We want to obey God, of course," my father said, "but we don't understand. This is so strange."

They clearly understood the pastor's words to mean that God was promising that their unborn child—their seventh—would grow up to serve Him. But no one in the Youssef family was a minister. My mother's family had worked in the building industry, and my father's family had been farmers. My dad worked for Shell Oil. My siblings had their sights set on banking, economics, and accounting.

Finally, my father said, "If God is in this, then we must obey."

"Letakon Masheato," said my mother. "May God's will be done." She was baffled by this promise as much as she was by the message not to abort. But as a devout Christian and a woman of prayer, she accepted the pastor's message as God's word to her.

The procedure was cancelled.

On September 25, 1948, Amerhome and Noza Youssef welcomed their seventh child into the world.

It was a boy.

They named him Michael. In Hebrew the word means, "Who is like God."

***

When I heard the full story of Pastor Girgis's intervention and my birth, I realized that even before I was born, God had a purpose and a plan for my life. I felt thankful, joyful, and quite special. But later, that same knowledge would torment me.

*Chapter Two*

## The Rebellious One

Throughout the months of her pregnancy, the doctor worried about my mother's health. But to the surprise of everyone, she had no problems during her pregnancy or delivery. After my birth, she became healthier and stronger than she had been in years. "I live by divine health," I remember her saying, although I didn't understand what she meant.

From the earliest days of my childhood, she and my father taught me about God. We were an evangelical Christian household. Our parents endeavored to lead us in prayer, and praying together at the family altar was a daily habit.

Because of my parents, I grew up having some sense of God, but I wasn't like my older brothers and sisters. Although I followed the family's Christian tradition, I always felt different. The others were renowned for their unquestioning obedience to the way we were brought up. But not me. From early childhood, I was the rebellious one.

My rebellion—in dozens of little ways—made me so much more difficult to cope with than my other siblings. Whereas the others obeyed when Father told them what to do, I often questioned his orders.

The real difference between the other children and me, however, became evident by the time I turned fifteen. I had grown bored with the church, and I didn't like what I called the "churchy" people. I still attended religious activities but with great reluctance. I never wanted to pray. And when it was to my advantage, I lied or misled my parents—a behavior that went against their religious instruction.

One time, I so angered and frustrated my mother that she hardly knew what to do. She warned me of my waywardness and hardened heart, but she realized her words were having no effect on me. I stood quietly, waiting for her to finish preaching so I could get out of the house and meet my fun-loving friends.

"You don't listen to what I say, Michael."

"I'm listening."

"No, Michael. You hear my words, but you don't listen," she said, as she launched into another lecture on my bad behavior.

I showed no remorse because I felt none.

In a final act of desperation, Mother laid her hand on my head and prayed, "Lord, if he's not going to be the one to serve You as I have believed all these years, then take him now."

For the first time, I grasped how badly my rebellious ways had hurt my parents, especially my mother. I don't recall how I reacted to her prayer, and the incident didn't make me change my ways, but I didn't forget it either.

By that time, I knew the details of my birth. I had often heard from the lips of my parents and older siblings that I was going to grow up to serve God. Maybe part of my rebellion was that I didn't like my future all planned for me. I felt that God hadn't given me a choice like He had for the rest of the family.

\*\*\*

Unlike my brothers, I wasn't a good student. I didn't study hard, and I barely scraped by from one school year to the next. My number-three brother, Samir, who became Undersecretary of Finance in Egypt, was as good with math as I was bad. He was the one I ran to for help in my studies, especially math.

Samir was a godly man. In my thinking, I was convinced he had never been a child. He had to have been born wise and righteous, and I often mocked him for those qualities. He was so scrupulous that he wouldn't use the pencil in his hand to help me because it belonged to the government and should only be used for government work. I would tease him, calling him "Mr. Holy Man" or "Goody Two-Shoes." Maybe I did that because, by comparison, his purity and honesty shined a glaring light on my mischievous ways.

Sometimes he would say, "Now you must promise to obey our parents," or, "You must promise you will not lie anymore."

"Yes, I promise," I would say. I was willing to promise anything to get help with math.

On one occasion when I asked him for help, he said, "Michael, I will make a bargain with you. I will help you with your math. In return, you will go with me to an evangelistic meeting at the Soul's Salvation Assembly."

"Oh, yes, certainly, Samir," I agreed. "Just help me with this page. Then I'll do whatever you want."

I had no intention of following through with my agreement, but that time, I couldn't renege as I usually did. Samir made it clear that if I did not go, he would not help me again. I decided it was worth sitting through a boring service to have his help available in the future. I would definitely need it. And although I didn't want to admit this even to myself, his love and sincerity made me feel guilty. On some level, I wanted to please him.

"Okay, I'll go," I said. "But as soon as the sermon is over, I am going to leave." Teen rebellion had brought about that attitude about sermons. When I was little, I loved to listen to them. Some I still remember.

"I won't argue about that," he said. "As long as you go and listen."

Listen was what I didn't want to do. In my miserable anticipation, I thought, *I know what I'll do. I'll go just like I promised, but I'll bring some of my friends. We'll laugh during the sermon and make the preacher mad.* My friends and I had behaved like that on several previous occasions.

That night, a Lebanese evangelist preached from the Old Testament book of Hosea. He spoke about God's patience with wayward children. I could feel his eyes boring into mine as he warned us, "One day God's patience will run out! You have a door open today. Enter through it. One day there will come a day of judgment. On that day, God's door will be shut."

As I listened to the evangelist, I forgot to laugh at him. It was the first time I had really listened to a preacher since I was a young boy. I can't explain what happened that evening, and there are some things no one can explain. I do know that every sentence seemed to speak to me. My friends sat beside me, but I don't know if they laughed or listened. I heard only the message being preached.

When the evangelist finished his sermon, he asked those of us who wanted to experience God's forgiveness to come forward. I was the first one to respond.

That night my life was changed forever.

On March 4, 1964, I finally surrendered my life to Jesus Christ. I was 16 years old.

Now, at last, I could say, "Thank You, God, for Your plan for my life."

***

By the time I was 16, my mother was in very bad health. She spent a lot of time in and out of medical facilities. Each time she went to the local hospital or one in Cairo, she came home a little weaker.

While my life was being transformed, my mother was in a Cairo hospital. Even though she would be coming home, I didn't want to wait for her to know that God had answered her prayers. So I wrote her a letter and told her everything.

At the end of the letter, I asked, "Will you forgive me for being such a rebellious son?"

As Nader told me later, she kept my letter under her pillow. She pulled it out to read so often that she memorized most of it. Whenever anyone came to visit in the hospital, she would reach under her pillow and pull out the letter. One time after sharing the letter, Mother told a visitor, "Now I can die in peace."

Four months later, my mother died.

After her death, I wondered if my rebellion had caused my mother to get worse. If I had not been so rebellious, would she still be alive? Was I to blame? It was a terrible burden for a young person to carry, and I didn't talk to anyone about it. I was afraid that if I did, they would tell me it was true.

In some ways, I still grieve over my mother's death. I know, however, that she died in God's time, and she died in victory. Only God's love and forgiveness enabled me finally to say, "If I contributed to her poor health, God has forgiven me and she has, too. I know she understands."

*Chapter Three*

## Directions

Now I was a Christian, and my life did change. The next four years were exciting, troublesome, and confusing. I often thought about the story of Pastor Girgis's intervention to save my life, and of his message that I would serve God's purpose. I had resented it before my conversion, but no longer. It now became a tremendous encouragement to me, and it increased my faith. I began to feel a strong sense of confidence that God's hand was indeed on me.

Yet I still thought like a normal teenager, and I wanted to make a decent living someday. Despite the message of Pastor Girgis, there were times when I didn't want to go into the ministry. Even though I was a Christian and had become active in our church, I kept saying, "I can serve Jesus Christ in an office as well as anywhere else." I believed my own words, for a time at least.

As a boy of 16, the economics of the ministry dismayed me. *These ministers of the gospel are poor people. Some of them struggle just to get by.* Although we had never been fabulously wealthy, I had never been poor, and I didn't want to be poor. The one consolation was if God did push me into the gospel ministry, He would provide for my needs.

The others in our family were successful. My father worked as a treasurer for Shell Oil—a company that mainly sold oil to gas stations and wheat mills, as well as propane gas to individual consumers. My industrious brothers were successful bankers or economists. My sisters were also either economics teachers or married accountants and bankers.

As the youngest boy, I naturally wanted to grow up to be just like my brothers. Unfortunately, it was obvious I couldn't be like them. They were all whizzes with numbers. No matter how hard I tried, I was not good at math, so that meant finance and economics were not options for me.

But despite my lack of aptitude with math, my family insisted that I go to engineering school. "You can do it," said Nathan, my second-eldest brother. "You need to put forth a more concerted effort." *Easy enough for him to say. He doesn't have to struggle the way I do.* Nathan was a bank president, and later he became a consultant with American Express Bank.

I hated engineering, and I didn't want to study it in college. But I admired my brothers, so I worked hard to please them. By the time I was ready to talk about college, I knew in my heart that God wanted me to preach, but I resisted considering such a call. I wasn't yet willing to face the future that God was laying out for me.

So I lived with God whispering in one ear, which I didn't want to hear, and my brothers talking in the other. The only way I could figure out how to escape a future in engineering was to enter the Air Force Academy. So when I finished high school, I applied to the academy and prayed, "God, please let them accept me. I don't have much chance of getting in, but you can do anything. Please do this for me." Amazing how we pray sometimes!

To everyone's amazement, I was accepted for enrollment in the Air Force Academy. Getting accepted made me the envy of my friends. Normally it took the influence of someone in high places for a student to get accepted (no one intervened for me that I am aware of). Because Egypt is a Muslim dominated nation, the academy selected less than 3 percent of their students from the Christian population. But I was one of them, and I was excited.

A position in the Air Force was a sought-after placement. After training, it would lead to a good salary and a career in the military. At the time, because Col. Nasser headed the government, the military was the ruling class of Egypt.

However, life didn't turn out to be that simple. When the opening day of the academy came, I didn't report because I didn't know about it. For some unknown reason, I had received the notification of acceptance but not one word about when I was to report. After I had received my letter of acceptance, I waited. Normally the academy sent a registered letter to the student with all pertinent information, but mine never came.

For nearly a month, I waited. When it still had not arrived, I went in person to the academy and asked, "When will I know my reporting date?"

"Report date? The incoming class started a week ago," the officer in charge said. "You're too late. You should have been here. You were notified by registered mail."

"No, that is not true," I said, "I never received any registered mail."

"Everyone was notified by registered mail! If you didn't show up, you are at fault."

"But, sir," I pleaded, "I tell you the truth. I've been waiting at home for you to inform me when I should report."

Because I insisted I had not received notification, and with the help of a family friend, Col. Nabeel, the officer said they would check the records. All their records, as well as those of the post office, showed that they had indeed mailed the letter. As they investigated further, they realized that they had no receipt with a signature to show that I had received it.

"What do I do? May I still enroll? Will you allow me to catch up?"

The man shook his head. "This is not possible. We chose the next applicant on the list. You are too late."

"What can I do then?" I asked. "I very much want to enroll in the Air Force."

"You have missed your chance," he said with a shrug, making it obvious he did not consider that his problem. "The only thing I can suggest is that you wait until next year and make a new application."

"Will I automatically be accepted?"

"No guarantee of that," he said and dismissed me.

As I left his office, I felt like my world had crashed. For weeks I had built my dreams around a career in the Air Force.

By the time I reached home, I knew for certain that waiting a year was not going to work. In my heart, I knew that God had intervened and prevented me from moving forward with my plan. At the time, however, I was blinded by my immediate desires and failed to appreciate God's hand of protection.

*Chapter Four*

## The First Step

Why didn't I enter the Air Force? Why didn't the registered letter reach me? Out of the hundreds of letters the academy sent out, mine was the only one not delivered. Wasn't that strange? What was God trying to teach me through that experience?

For several days I desperately searched my heart. Why had I remained so rebellious? Why did I try to get into the Air Force when deep down I knew God had other plans for me? Gradually, I began to accept that I had demanded my own way once again. God had answered my prayer; I had been accepted. Then God lovingly slammed the door.

After a few weeks, I was well past my confusion. By then I could understand that God was saying, "Michael, this is not what I want for you. Don't wait and apply next year."

But I still wasn't ready to accept the path He wanted for me. My life was a living contradiction. I would cry to God for help, but at the same time rebel against His plan.

I would pray, "Thank you for keeping me out of the Air Force. I'll do whatever you want me to do. It's up to you to show me what you want." I would mean that prayer, more than any other before. But when I wouldn't get an answer after several days, my faith would waver. Despite my sincere intentions, I remained anything but a committed disciple. So because I had no strong sense of direction and no dramatic push from God, I did the only thing I knew to do. I enrolled in a telecommunications engineering school—that way I could buy some time and please my family.

I started my classes, yet something was not right. Inwardly I knew I wasn't giving my life fully to God. But if being in telecommunications school wasn't where I belonged, what should I do? Where *did* I belong? Finally, the mental anguish became so overpowering that I began to pray about my future again. For several days I talked to God, and I surrendered myself. I promised that this time, I would do only what He wanted, no matter what it was or where He wanted me to go.

During a period of several days, I began to feel that God was calling me to prepare for a preaching ministry. Along with that came a strong conviction that God had called me into a ministry *not in Egypt*.

"If not Egypt, where God?"

"The United States," came back the answer.

Nearly every student wanted to study in the United States. But my chances of getting accepted to a U.S. school were somewhere between nonexistent and impossible. I was definitely open to the idea, however. Although I had applied to the Air Force Academy to avoid engineering, I hated the Nasser regime with its socialistic ideals and its recent Six-Day War with Israel, which had brought our nation to its knees.

I didn't hear more from God, but in my heart I knew the answer. *I was to leave Egypt.* God would open the door at the right time. No matter how impossible it seemed at the moment, I had a deep assurance that I would receive my training in a country other than Egypt.

For several weeks nothing happened, and I agonized over the lack of direction. Had I really heard God speak? I didn't know anyone in America, so how could I get there? As I continued to pray, however, a feeling grew that God would indeed lead me out of Egypt, but not directly to the United States—that would come later. "All right, God," I said. "It doesn't matter where or when, because I am willing to go anywhere you take me."

I surrendered, but I didn't understand how God could possibly work this out.

The conviction to leave grew within me, but I still didn't know how to go about it. I decided to put God to the test, to find out if He had been speaking to me. "God," I prayed, "if you are truly calling me to study abroad, you have to help me. If this is your plan and you will guide me, I promise that I won't stay here."

By 1968, life had become extremely difficult in Egypt, especially for Christians. Nationalism was on the rise and contempt for Christians was increasing. The Six-Day War had taken place in May 1967. The world called it the Six-Day War because that's exactly how long it lasted, and my country of birth had suffered deep humiliation from Israel's attacks. Then came the big blow that affected me—Nasser decreed that all students, when they finished high school or college, had to enroll in the National Service. The country was preparing to fight Israel again.

By then, I had grown in my Christian understanding. I was grateful to God for keeping me out of the Air Force Academy. Besides, I opposed war with Israel. Like many others, I felt that Egypt was floundering. *I don't want to go to war and get killed defending Palestinians against Israel.* I had strong views on the Arab foolishness of wanting to throw Israel into the sea.

By that time, I knew that I did not want to fight, and I especially did not want to enroll for military call-up. But I couldn't break the law and refuse to serve. What could I do?

I did what I had learned by example from my mother—I prayed and fasted. My praying and going without food went on for several days. Almost by the hour, the certainty grew that God was leading me to emigrate from Egypt.

*But how do I leave?*

For the next several weeks I didn't attend my school classes. Instead, I used the time to make the rounds to the foreign embassies. The first one I went to, the American Embassy, had been closed because of the Six-Day War. Canada was no longer accepting immigrants. But when I visited the Australian Embassy, they told me, "Yes, we are still accepting immigrants."

Hardly able to believe the good news, I asked for an application. Right on the spot, I filled in the information. I needed a sponsor, however. My brother, Nathan, had a friend in Australia, so after I returned home, Nathan contacted him and he agreed to sponsor me. With that obstacle overcome, I returned to the Australian Embassy. They put me through a physical examination, and then I had to go through a number of interviews. After more than six months, the Australian Embassy notified me that I had been accepted for immigration to their country and a visa was authorized.

"Everything is in order, Mr. Youssef. You must now obtain a passport and your prepaid ticket to Australia. At that time, we shall give you a visa to enter Australia."

"Thank you! Thank you!" I left the Embassy greatly excited.

And then, once again, my plans fell apart. The very day the Australians told me I could immigrate, a new ruling came out from

Mr. Nasser: No university student could hold a passport or travel abroad.

"God, I tried to emigrate because I felt you were leading me in that direction. Now I can't leave Egypt. What is going on? How could you allow this to happen? Why didn't you delay Nasser's ruling until I got out?"

I couldn't understand why He would allow the law to change on that very day. Why not change it a week later? Then it wouldn't have mattered.

"Oh, God," I cried out, "I prayed for guidance. I had my hopes raised. Everything seemed to be working out. Now you slam the door in my face. What do I do now?"

No matter how much I tried to find peace, I felt only confusion. Again I searched my heart, asking, "Have I misunderstood your will, God?" The situation did not make sense. As I would later understand, and after I had faced many more obstacles, the memory of that disappointment would turn out to offer an invaluable learning experience.

I prayed for a long time, and slowly a sense of peace began to calm my agitated state. Circumstances had not changed, yet I knew everything was going to work out all right. Two sentences kept coming into my mind again and again: "Just pray. I will intervene."

"I believe you," I said, "I'm going to do that. I promise to pray until you intervene. I can't see how you'll do it, but I'm going to trust you and obey."

When my friends and neighbors realized that I persisted in believing I would go to Australia, most of them didn't understand what was happening to me. Even some of the Christians thought I might be losing it. One of them asked, "Are you really serious, Michael? How can you pray for God to help you change the law?"

I didn't argue, but I felt their scorn. However, it didn't seem to matter. God was with me. That's what really counted.

One reason my friends responded that way was because of the conditions we lived under. Fear had spread throughout the country. No one knew what was going to happen next. We heard rumors of a military buildup by Israel and its allies. Others whispered that all the Arab nations were going to rally together to crush Israel. Every day it seemed that new, fearful information was circulated. The stories bred misunderstanding and apprehension. War and restrictions were on everyone's mind.

Although I had God's peace in my heart, for a long time nothing happened. For weeks I continued to pray, yet no door opened. Still young in the faith, I didn't understand why God was taking so long. At one point I cried out, "God, why don't you do something? I can't escape. I can't even get a passport. Yet whenever I pray, I'm still convinced you want me to leave Egypt." I felt like a bird locked inside a cage. I continued to pray because it was my only option, but I was growing impatient.

Then a door opened—so slightly I didn't realize it at first.

*Chapter Five*

**Through a Different Door**

Hope came from Beirut, Lebanon, when I received an invitation from a good friend who lived there. He and I had met during my first days at the engineering school. He knew I wanted to leave Egypt, so he had told me, "When I get home, I'll send you an invitation to visit."

I appreciated his saying that. Despite his promise, however, I had no assurance he would follow through. Until the day I held his letter in my hands, I worried that he would forget or change his mind. To add to the stress, even if he did invite me, there was no guarantee that I could get out of the country.

He did follow through. My friend's letter was a formal invitation to visit Beirut for a week. Although the invitation read, "visit," he knew in issuing it, and I knew in receiving it, that he was being used as an instrument to provide me an opportunity to study in Beirut—if I could get out of Egypt.

"Thank you, God," I said, as tears streamed down my cheeks. Still I had no idea how I was going to reach Beirut, but I knew this was God's answer.

As my friend well knew, if people wanted to visit another county, especially an Arab country, for a week or less, they would be considered for an exit visa.[1] *If*—and that was always the uncertain element—*if* I could get an exit visa, I could apply for a passport. However, in order to get the visa, I had to go in person to the Ministry of War.

Of course, my family knew that once I got out of Egypt, I wasn't coming back.

Although that saddened them, they stood with me and believed it was what I had to do. By now they had all realized I was preparing myself for ministry, and they rejoiced with me. I told my friends about the invitation to spend a week in Lebanon. I'm sure some of them understood that I was talking about leaving for good, but I never discussed that possibility with anyone.

"Don't even bother trying to get an exit visa," one of my friends said. "It won't do any good."

"You're liable to end up in the army before you leave the building," said another.

"Or in jail!" added a third.

"Just give up the idea. God will work out something," most of them counseled.

Despite the lack of encouragement, I knew in my heart that the invitation to Lebanon was God's way of answering my prayer and providing a way for me to leave Egypt. Even though I believed, I was scared. The things my friends said affected me, but their warnings didn't stop me.

I went to the administrative offices of the Ministry of War. There I learned that a particular general was the one who had the authority to sign my request. "Where is his office?" I asked.

The receptionist pointed, but added, "I can tell you right now that you are wasting your time."

---

[1] Lebanon, although it used to be predominantly a "Christian" nation, it was considered an Arab country.

"Thank you," I told him, "but I must try." Refusing to turn back, I got to the general's outer office, but his aide would not let me in to see him. "Please," I said, and explained what I wanted. "It will take only a few minutes."

"You may not see the general," he insisted. "Even if you could, I assure you that you won't get it approved."

"Then let me go in and find out for myself."

Although I tried every form of persuasion I could think of, he refused to let me see him. Finally, knowing I was defeated, I left. I returned the next day and went through the same procedure. I did that again and again for several weeks. I determined to keep on, no matter how long it took. If God was opening this door, I had to do everything I could to go through it. Besides, I had come this far, so I wasn't going to quit now.

Finally, on a Sunday morning, shortly before seven, and after having prayed all night, I went back again. While I talked with the general's aide for several minutes, one of the guards, who must have been listening, walked over to the desk. "What is the trouble?"

"The general won't grant any student an exit visa." The aide nodded at me and glared, "Not for any reason."

"I have this request," I said as I pulled out the letter. "It is a request to visit Beirut for one week. Surely, he can allow this."

"The general has said no one gets out!" replied the young Lieutenant. "It's government regulations."

"Who does the general think he is, God himself?" the guard said, as he turned to me and smiled. "You go on through. Go in there and see the general." He pointed to the door and stared at the secretary, defying him to object.

"Thank you," I said as I hurried past and knocked on the door. Even before I knocked, I could hear the general's voice on the telephone. He was using some of the foulest language, which was common for military people in Egypt. I knocked anyway, and without waiting for an answer, went inside. It was a huge office, and he stood behind a massive desk. The whole atmosphere was very intimidating.

He glanced up at me and yelled in a deep, harsh voice, "What in the blankety-blank do you want?" He wore the uniform of an army general. As I already knew, Nasser had placed many of those generals to enforce discipline within the military because so many soldiers had deserted during the Six-Day War.

I stared at him, praying for courage.

"Well? What do you want?"

I stepped forward and showed him my application. "You are stupid," he yelled as he grabbed it from my hand and dropped it on the corner of his desk. "I know you and your kind. Don't you think I know why you're here? You're trying to escape national service. I know exactly what you're trying to do. I know your type." He ranted for several minutes. Finally he paused and picked up my application. "Michael! Michael!" My name was recognizable as Christian. "And you dare to come here! You all are nothing but scheming traitors!"

I said nothing; I was too scared. My body was shaking like a leaf on a tree on a windy day. My mouth was dry. Fear crawled through me. While he ranted, I prayed silently, "Lord, this isn't the answer to prayer that I was looking for. Please do something. You sent me here, so You have to help me."

He threw the application at me and I picked it up.

"I can send you to a place where no one will ever find you again! You can't run away from your duty and your responsibility to your country. You think I don't know—"

# Leading The Way in W.V.

| Station | Day | Time |
|---|---|---|
| Cornerstone | Sunday | 2:30 a.m. & 8:30 a.m. |
| | Monday | 8:00 a.m. |
| Daystar | Saturday | 7:00 a.m. |
| | Sunday | 9:30 p.m. |
| Discovery Channel | Sunday | 7:30 a.m. |
| DBN | Sunday | 7:00 p.m. |
| The Church Channel | Sunday | 9:00 a.m. |

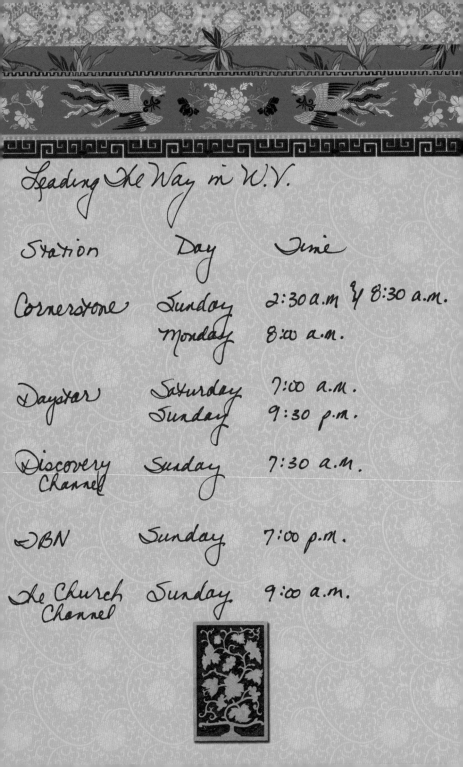

In the middle of his bombastic yelling, another general barged in. He didn't acknowledge me, but just walked past me, cutting off the general in mid-sentence. Some problem had developed with a particular officer, and they started to discuss it as if I no longer existed.

In their heated discussion, they seemed to have forgotten about me. The sensible thing to do was ease out of the office and go home. He had me so frightened, I was afraid that if I provoked him anymore, he would send me to jail.

Cautiously I took one step backward. Neither man paid any attention. I was debating on whether to back all the way to the door or just turn around and walk out. Just then the visitor looked my way and said, "What does this young man want?"

"He wants an exit visa to visit Lebanon. That's what he wants! He is a stupid boy!"

"Oh, let him go."

"What do you mean?"

"Just let him go." The visiting general turned to me and held out his hand and beckoned for my application. "Give it here, son." He signed it and then stamped it. "Son, go. Get out of here."

I couldn't leave fast enough. As I walked out the door, I didn't know whether I was alive or dead. *Is this just a dream? Should I pinch myself?* I flashed my approval at the young Lieutenant and waved it at the guard and smiled as I headed for the front of the building, not wanting to slow down and get called back to the general's office.

Once outside, I walked across the street and sat down on a park bench. My body was shaking. I was perspiring. I felt so sick; the queasiness of my stomach made me want to vomit. Then I stared at the paper in my hand. The signature and the stamp were there. *God has done the impossible. I just needed to trust and obey.*

31

I hurried over to the passport office and submitted the application, and they cleared me for a passport—which I had to pay for and pick up the next day.

When I returned the following day, the officer said, "You must leave Egypt within 48 hours. If you do not, the passport and exit visa are automatically revoked."

Only two days? How could I leave so quickly? I hadn't packed or made a plane reservation. I had assumed it would take weeks. Nor had it occurred to me that there would be such a time restriction. But the instructions were clear: I had to fly out in two days or I could never leave.

With my passport in hand, I went to the offices of Egypt Airlines to book my ticket. The agent shook her head, "I am sorry, that is impossible. All flights are booked for the next six days."

"But I can't wait that long." I showed her my passport and exit visa.

"This is a religious holiday period," she said, meaning an Islamic holiday. It was obvious that she was not going to do anything to help me.

"But I need only one seat."

"Yes, of course, but hundreds of others have come ahead of you. They also wish only one seat. And some of them have been waiting for weeks for a cancellation."

Dejectedly I walked away. "God, what do I do now?" As soon as I said those words, I thought of a Christian friend who worked for Egypt Air Lines. I immediately went to his office.

He confirmed what the ticket agent had said. "This is the best I can do for you. I'll put your name on the waiting list. I'll move it as close to the top as I can. You are to go to the airport tomorrow, and be there by 4:00 A.M. It is the last flight to get you out in time.

Beyond my doing that, God has to take over if He wants you to leave."

That night I agonized in prayer, asking God for assurance and peace. "I know you are teaching me to trust and obey. Now make a way where there is no way . . . again."

My sister, Eva, who had been a prayer intercessor for me for years, came to Cairo to see me off. Then at 3:00 A.M., three of my siblings took me to the airport.

"Are you sure it is worthwhile to wait?" one of them asked.

"I don't know if I'll be able to fly out or not," I said, "but I know it is worthwhile." At the time I was thinking, *What else can I do? If God wants me to leave Egypt, I'll get on that plane. If not, then surely He will open a different door.*

***

As the plane began to load, I looked at the vast number of people milling around. I was afraid to count them, but it seemed there were more people than could possible fit into one plane.

Finally the last person was checked in. Then the real wait came. A crowd was still gathered around, clutching their luggage, obviously waiting and listening for their names to be called. A flight attendant came out, said something to the gate agent, shook her head, and went back to the plane. I was afraid to look at anyone. I continued to pray silently, "God, You have brought me so far, You will have to make a way for me. This is my only chance."

Finally, a voice called out my full name, "Michael Amerhome Youssef."

I was so overjoyed at hearing my name that I don't remember what, if anything, I said to my family members. I do remember running to the gate as if the airline personnel might change their minds. As I thanked the gate agent, he said, "You are one very lucky person, you know that?"

"Lucky?"

"You see those people?" He pointed to at least twenty others waiting for news that they were allowed on the plane. When I nodded, he said, "We have one seat available because somebody either canceled or didn't show up. You are so lucky to be at the top of the waiting list."

As I sat in the bus that took me to the plane, I knew it wasn't luck at all. It was God's powerful and sovereign hand working out the details.

One hour later, I landed in Beirut.

*Chapter Six*

**One Step Closer**

On February 4, 1969, I arrived in Beirut and immediately fell in love with the city. At that time, Beirut was known as one of the most scenic places in the world. Located on the eastern Mediterranean coast, its picturesque setting was sheltered by the beautiful hills around it.

My friend who had originally invited me to Lebanon was back in Cairo, but I still had several contacts in the city, including the evangelist who had led me to the Lord four years earlier. He introduced me to a single pastor named Khaliel Ibrahaim, who invited me to stay in his house for a while.

I had come to Beirut to do one thing—to study for the ministry. On the advice of some friends, I attended a Bible school for a few months. The more I studied the Bible courses, the more at peace I became about my future. I was doing the right thing in preparing for the ministry, and from that time on, not a doubt entered my mind or heart. "This is where I belong," I said again and again.

For the first time, I understood why I had always felt different from my siblings. They were Christians attuned to making their witness known in the business world. My way was to be more overt with my words. I wanted to reach those outside the faith, and

I knew my place to serve God was within the leadership of the church.

I missed my family, but I had a new kind of family—brothers and sisters in Jesus Christ. Most of all, I had the peace of God and the assurance that this was the first big step God had planned for me. Yet at no time did I believe that Beirut was to be the end of my journey. Having felt that way all along, I went to the Australian Embassy and asked them to request my file and visa from their embassy in Cairo.

Everything in Beirut was progressing well. It would have been the ideal place to live, if I had felt like that was God's plan. For me, life was harmonious. My studies challenged both my brain and my spirit. I felt totally content, and I decided that when God was ready for me to take the next step, I would know. Until then, I would enjoy where I was.

Then, God directed me onward.

After I had been in Beirut for several months, one of my older brothers, Nathan, sent me a message. Part of it read something like this: "Leave as soon as possible, Michael. Do not stay, or I shall come there to make sure you do not stay."

Nathan's concern was for my safety. From the beginning of my studies, he felt I had no future in Lebanon. War had not broken out there, but he knew it was only a matter of time before the country exploded with violence. Palestinian refugees were growing in number. Islamic fundamentalists were rising to positions of power—all were people who resented a Christian president and the few wealthy men at the top. That created a strong climate for disaster. It was time to leave, my brother said.

Get out of Beirut? Emotionally that was easy enough to consider. Although I liked living there, I was ready when God led me. Getting out of Lebanon would present no problem. But then what?

So I was overjoyed the day the Australian Embassy called to inform me that my file had been received. Everything was in order, and they had arranged for my exit papers. "You are welcome to immigrate to Australia."

I was ecstatic.

Then reality set in. I had one serious problem.

I needed money.

How could I pay for the airline ticket? At that time, it cost $500 for a one-way flight to Australia. Back in 1969, for a student like me to raise $500 would have been like raising $5,000 today. My family couldn't send that much money out of Egypt; it was illegal. Several times they had managed to send me small amounts of cash with friends who passed through Beirut, but that was all they could do. And I didn't have the opportunity to earn it. I was a student, just barely scraping by.

Again, I turned to God. "Lord, You have opened this door. Surely You are not going to let something as small as money stop me from taking the next step." I meant those words. Almost immediately, peace filled my heart, because I knew God would provide for me.

More than once I pleaded with the travel broker to allow me to pay once I reached Australia, but he wanted to take advantage of me and make every cent off me that he could. "Cash only," he said.

"But I promise to repay as soon as I can get settled."

"Without money in my hands," he said, "I can do nothing for you."

Finally, a Christian friend guaranteed my loan for the travel broker. I promised my friend, "I will work night and day to pay this money back."[2] The travel agent was all smiles when he issued my ticket.

\*\*\*

I arrived in Sydney, Australia, on Sunday morning via British Airways (BOAC), a flight that seemed to take forever. Along the way, the plane stopped in Bombay and Vietnam. Many GIs from Vietnam got on board.

Although I didn't know anyone in Australia, my brother Nathan had written to the man who initially sponsored me and asked if he would pick me up at the airport. Nathan gave him my arrival time and flight. He also asked if I could stay with him for a few days. I left before we had a chance to get an answer. Would he meet me? I didn't know. But I did know that one way or another, God would provide. All I needed to do was trust and obey.

\*\*\*

It was a strange feeling to exit from the plane. In some ways I felt like Abraham of old, who left his homeland and traveled like a nomad at God's leading. Like Abraham, I knew God was leading me.

When I landed, I had the equivalent of 100 American dollars in my pocket—borrowed—and one small suitcase. "I am in your hands, God," I said as I entered the terminal. "You are responsible for my being here, so I trust you to provide for me." Those weren't just words; they came from an inner peace that made me know I was in His perfect will.

"Michael?" asked a man in heavily-accented English. "Michael Amerhome Youssef?"

I smiled, knowing it was my brother's friend.

"I am Wagi Solomon. I have been waiting for you."

---

[2]    Once I settled in Australia, it took me six months to save enough to repay the loan.

"Thank you," I said. And then I sent a quick cable to Heaven. "How can I thank you for taking care of all these details?"

Wagi and his wife took me to their home, told me that I could stay as long as needed, and that they would help me in any way possible.

I was grateful to God and to them. I was now one step closer to the United States.

*Chapter Seven*

## One Step at a Time

I was a stranger in a strange land, with few contacts, and no assurances of work or continuing my biblical training. Other than Wagi Solomon, no one in Australia knew me. I went because that was the door God had opened. I landed on that island continent with nothing but a few personal belongings.

The only other things in my possession were two letters of introduction. The first was written by Aubrey Whitehouse, head of the Lebanon Bible Institute in Beirut. The second letter was written by Ken Bailey, who had been a good friend of our family for many years. He was a professor of Greek New Testament at the Near East School of Theology in Beirut. Both letters were recommendations about my character and commitment to Jesus Christ, and they urged my acceptance at Moore Theological College.

My Christian background was becoming complex. In Egypt, I had been a member of the Coptic Evangelical "Presbyterian" Church. In Lebanon, I had attended Baptist and Assemblies of God churches. Now I was being recommended to enter an Anglican school. My two friends who wrote the letters had essentially said, "Forget the church label. If you're looking for a solidly evangelical, biblical training college, you need to enter Moore. It is the most evangelical school in Australia." They addressed their letters to Don Robinson, who was vice principal of the seminary (and who would later become the Archbishop of Sydney).

On Monday morning, the day after I had arrived, I got directions from Mr. Solomon, took a bus and a train, and went to the home of Don Robinson on the campus of Moore College. Looking back, it sounds presumptuous to knock on his door at 8:30 a.m. and present myself and my two letters without warning, but it was the only form of approach I knew.

Dr. Robinson was extremely kind. God gave me favor in his eyes. He understood my situation, and I didn't have to talk about lack of money or other problems. That morning, he sent me over to meet Ken Churchwood, a local rector in the suburb of Kingsgrove where I had been staying with Wagi. The next day, Ken took me out to find a job. I was hired immediately as a technical assistant for the telecommunications department of what was then part of the Australia Post, the government postal service. As a technical assistant, I would mostly be welding wires and doing light technical work in a telephone exchange.

Life had suddenly sped up. I had arrived in a strange country on Sunday morning, and I reported for work on Wednesday at 7:00 a.m. Saturday, I rented my own apartment and moved in. My heart overflowed with thanks. All my needs were being met.

Because Ken Churchwood and his people had been so kind to me, I decided to worship at their church, St. Thomas Kingsgrove.

At the end of the worship service on my third Sunday in Australia, Ken's wife, Betty, pulled me aside. "I would like you to meet some of our members." She introduced me as "Michael Youssef, who has just emigrated from Egypt and will soon enter Moore College to prepare for the ministry here in Australia."

I didn't correct her. As much as I liked the country and its people, I knew Australia was just one more step in my ultimate journey to the United States. I had come to Australia to study for the ministry. Almost as soon as I had surrendered my life to prepare for ministry, deep within, I knew that America would be my base for a global ministry.

Mrs. Churchwood introduced me to a number of people, most of them older members. Among the charming people I met was Loran Bailey, a remarkably friendly woman.

"Do you have somewhere to go for lunch?" Mrs. Bailey asked.

"No, actually, I don't."

"Would you like to come with us? We would love to have you."

"Yes, that would be nice." I was thinking it would be refreshing to visit with an Australian family. But just as I accepted, I saw a momentary panic in her eyes. As I learned later, only then did she realize she had nothing prepared to feed me.

"I'll have to run on home," she said, recovering quickly. "I'll have my daughter walk you to the house, because I need to go right away." She left immediately. The minister's wife took me to meet Mrs. Bailey's daughter.

"This is Elizabeth Bailey," she said, introducing me to a lovely red-haired woman. After a few words to get us acquainted, Mrs. Churchwood excused herself and mingled with others. As Elizabeth and I chatted, I couldn't stop staring at her.

After a few minutes, Elizabeth said, "Let's go then, shall we?"

Honestly, I remember little of what either of us said. But one thing I do know. During the short time it took Elizabeth to walk me to their house, I fell in love with her. It started with her eyes, a beautiful shade of green. But as well as her physical looks, her intelligence impressed me. As I learned later, she was a year older than me. That was no problem. In fact, from childhood, all my friends seemed to be older. Perhaps it was because I grew up as the youngest boy in a family of eight children. In school, I often felt I didn't know how to communicate with people my age.

Elizabeth had recently graduated from college and was teaching French at the local high school. Her grasp of linguistics impressed me immensely. Besides French, she taught German and Italian. When we talked about world conditions, she seemed remarkably aware and informed, not isolated as many Australians I met later. Mostly, I just enjoyed talking with her.

The afternoon I spent with the Bailey family was the most beautiful time in my life since childhood. I had been lonelier for my family in Egypt than I had realized, and the warmth and acceptance from this family did much to ease that loneliness. From the first moment in their home, I knew I was in the presence of a loving and godly family. Her parents were kind and thoughtful. I later learned that Elizabeth's older brother died two years earlier in a car accident.

Although I was already madly in love with Elizabeth that first day, of course I didn't say anything about how I felt. I did ask her for a date and she accepted. After that, we began to do things together at church. Three or four weeks passed before I told her that I cared for her. She admitted that she liked me a great deal.

Our lives were progressing nicely together until one night six weeks after we had started dating. We had been to a party together. On the way back to her house, she said, "Michael, what is your life's plan?"

"Eventually, I plan to go to the United States."

She didn't say anything for a few minutes. When she did, it was absolutely the last thing I had expected to hear. "Then I think it would be best if we stopped seeing each other."

"Why?" I asked. "I like you very much and—"

"I can't go to the United States. I'm now an only child. My parents have already lost a son. They're getting older. I have to be here if they need me."

We talked a long time, but no matter what I said, it still came back to the same point. I felt God was directing me eventually to the United States. Elizabeth was committed to remain in Australia to be near her parents.

We broke up. The breakup was devastating to both of us. During the next several weeks, we were both miserable and missed each other. Then, five weeks later, I sent her flowers on her birthday. The next day she called to thank me.

"I've missed you," I said.

"I've missed you, too."

"I would like us to get together again." Before she could object, I said, "Let's take it one step at a time and allow God to guide us. We won't have to worry about the future."

"Yes, all right," she said. "We'll trust God to show us."

We started to date again.

We did take it one step at a time. The wall between us crumbled. We had not resolved the matter of the United States, but we knew we were both following God's will. I proposed, and we became engaged in March 1971, just ten months after arriving in Australia. In December, we were married.

In the meantime, I worked and studied so I could complete the equivalency of the university matriculation, which I did by the end of 1971. In February, I enrolled at Moore Theological College.[3] Three years later, I was ordained by the Anglican Diocese of Sydney.

---

[3] In Australia, the academic year goes from February to November.

While I was in college, I worked part time at Holy Trinity Anglican Church in Dulwich Hill, but the income barely paid for my books. Elizabeth retained her job teaching French. It was hard for me to see her working to support us. Many males have that problem, but especially coming from my culture, that type of thing just wasn't done. Women could work, or course, but not to support the family.

So I made Elizabeth a promise. "Once I've finished my education and get a position, I promise that you won't have to work outside of the home, again."

We wanted children, and both of us agreed that she needed to be at home while they were young.

By God's grace I was able to keep that promise.

*Chapter Eight*

## Different Steps

I struggled academically during my seminary years. I had to work harder in my first year at seminary than I did later when I studied for a doctoral degree. There were three reasons.

The first problem, of course, was that English was still a foreign language to me. Second, Moore College was recognized as one of the most demanding theological schools in the world. They maintained an extremely high academic level. Solidly orthodox and evangelical, their standards were the highest possible. Never having been a good student in Egypt, I did not become transformed overnight.

Third, we had several extremely bright people in our particular class. Three of them later became professors at the school. Today, my fellow students are all in leadership positions with the Diocese in Sydney. Frankly, although I admired them, they intimidated me. They were so brilliant that I often felt inadequate when they made their theological arguments.

For me, however, the worst part of seminary was learning New Testament Greek. For the final examination, we were given a portion of the New Testament to translate from Greek to English. Then we had to take a different passage and translate it backward from English to Greek. From Greek to English, I did all right. But when it came to translating from English to Greek, I just couldn't seem to do it. I had to take Greek twice.

It wasn't that languages were so hard for me. After all, when I was in school in Egypt, we had to study English from grades seven through twelve. In tenth grade we started learning French. So I had studied French for a few years, and English for six.

Of course, learning a language in school and speaking it are two very different things. Back in Egypt, I had received the most help with English by getting to know several Canadians and Americans. While still a boy, I used every chance to practice on them. They laughed at my mistakes, but they tried to help me speak correctly. By the time I got to Australia, I still wasn't fluent in English, but I was able to make myself understood.

As in the British system, everything ultimately depended on finals, called external examinations. How students did during the year actually had no bearing on the results. Someone could sail brilliantly through every class and still fail the externals.

In my case, I even surprised a particular professor who didn't want me to go on. By the grace of God, I did better than pass my exams; I actually scored quite high.

\*\*\*

Yes, I struggled academically, but I kept studying. As I studied my way through seminary, I reminded myself that God had called me, and God would help me. The best part of being a seminarian was that I had opportunities to preach in churches on Sundays. Although the branch church at Holy Trinity was the main church I preached at, because of my background, I was invited to be a guest speaker at many other churches. Each time, as I stood before the people and spoke, I knew that was where I belonged.

Rectors were able to guide, correct, and advise me. I learned to be a better preacher. I got the experience of working with a small congregation, and I especially valued the practical experience of ministering to older people and shut-ins. That first year also gave me the opportunity to do a lot of evangelism. I was able to share the good news of Jesus Christ with many members of that parish who had never surrendered their lives to Jesus.

***

After my ordination in February 1975, I accepted a call as an assistant rector at St. Philips Caringbah in a suburb of Sydney.

During my undergraduate and seminary days, Elizabeth continued to teach. But once I went to St. Philips, I kept my promise. Now I had a job, so she wouldn't have to work again.

At St. Philips I worked as a curate (the assistant to the rector) for two years. I loved being there. If God had not been nudging me to move on, I would have been content to stay at St. Philip's indefinitely. I loved the people. Elizabeth and I became quite close to the members. In fact, nearly 40 years later, we still keep in touch with several of them. When they visit the United States, they make it a point to stay with us.

No matter how much I enjoyed being at St. Philip's and no matter how thoroughly I enjoyed the work, I always had an inner sense that God was leading me onward. I knew the United States was my next step. I didn't hear a voice, have a vision, or experience anything of a supernatural nature. But I did have a sense that God had something special for me to do, and I knew that I would enter into that special work only after I went to America.

Although I had no doubt God was calling me to the United States, I didn't know exactly why. The sense of calling was so strong that it felt almost like a compulsion at times. On a few occasions, when the feeling became so powerful, I asked, "God, is this from you? Or is it just the allure of America that keeps pulling me? If it's your will for me, then you will have to provide the way."

Certainly that desire did not come from dissatisfaction with my life in Australia. Living in Sydney was about as good as I could have expected life to be. Yet, dissatisfaction tugged at my heart. I felt I needed more opportunity to learn. That seemed strange to contemplate. After all, I am not what you would call an academic. Yet I had studied theology and now had a good grasp of the Bible. As fine as my seminary instruction was, I felt I needed a better sense of how to communicate, especially cross-culturally.

I had already lived in three different cultures: Egyptian, Lebanese, and Australian. Each move had been a shock to me, and yet I managed to adapt. I had a strong urge to prepare myself to preach to people of many cultures. Although I didn't voice it to anyone, not even Elizabeth, I was already beginning to feel that God had a plan for me that included communicating across cultural and national boundaries. Yet it did seem strange. What kind of ministry would that be? I didn't know anyone else who did that.

When I finally shared my burden with Elizabeth, she said, "Michael, I am with you wherever God leads." Tears were in her eyes when she spoke those words, knowing that would mean leaving her native land and her aging parents. "God is first in our lives," she said. "We need to trust him and obey."

After much prayer and inner turmoil, I applied for admission to the School of World Mission at Fuller Theological Seminary in Pasadena, California. I wanted to study cross-culture communication with Professor Paul Hiebert. When I sent off my application, Elizabeth and I prayed, "God, if you want us there, they will have to accept Michael into the graduate program."

Less than a month later, a letter of acceptance arrived. They also offered me the possibility of financial assistance. It was the sign we had waited for.

Elizabeth and I rejoiced, giving thanks to God for showing us the next step.

Everything was perfect.

*Chapter Nine*

## A Man Named John

Isn't it amazing how things that seem like little consequence at the time can develop into life-changing events? We don't have any idea at the time, and yet, God is at work. I want to tell you about one such life-changing event in my life.

One day while I was ministering at St. Philip's, I received a telephone call from a lady named Ivanka. She was a Roman Catholic who lived in the parish, and she had never met me. Ivanka was the public relations director for an international corporation. Her boss was an American Christian who served on the board of the Haggai Institute—an organization I had never heard of.

As she related to me later, my involvement had begun when her boss told her, "I want to get in contact with several ministers in Sydney and have them meet John Haggai. They need to know what he's doing on the international scene. Perhaps some of them would like to get involved."

John Haggai was planning to visit Sydney in 1976.

"I don't know any ministers," she said, "but let me check it out." Being an excellent public relations person, she asked around and heard my name mentioned several times. She went back to her employer with the information she had gathered. "Michael

Youssef of St. Philips sounds as if he might be exactly the type of person you're looking for."

So she called me on the phone. After she introduced herself and explained where she worked, she said, "I'd like to invite you to a dinner."

"Why would you want me to come to dinner? What is this all about? You don't even know me."

"True, but we have a number of mutual contacts," she said. "By the way, have you ever heard of John Haggai?"

I admitted that I hadn't.

"Well, Dr. Haggai is an Arab evangelist, and he's—"

"Haggai is a Jewish name," I said, and laughed. "What do you mean he's an *Arab* evangelist?"

"I may have that part wrong," she said, "but I do know what this man is doing in the world. He is training national leaders in virtually every third-world country."

"Sounds fine, but I'll have to decline," I said. "Right now I have so much work that I don't have time for such meetings."

I spoke the truth. I *was* too busy, working an average of 80 hours a week. But that wasn't the major reason. American evangelists often came to Australia. Most of them tried to raise money for crusades and evangelistic meetings. I didn't want to get caught up in trying to be a fund-raiser for some American evangelist I had never heard of.

To her credit, Ivanka didn't give up. She called me a week later and again invited me to dinner. "No, thank you," I said.

A few days later, Ivanka called a third time and finally a fourth time. Like the judge that Jesus spoke about in one of his parables, I finally accepted her invitation.

Soon after that, I attended a formal dinner where John Haggai was the guest of honor. He told us about himself and his vision to provide leadership training around the world. He was a man of medium height and build, dark complexion, and he spoke with a strong voice that really moved me. *This man is different. He knows which people he wants to reach, and he's going after them. His vision is exciting!*

During the few days John Haggai was in Australia, we became good friends. The following year, John returned to Australia, and I asked him to preach at my church and share the vision of the Haggai Institute. I also arranged for him to speak at several other churches.

After one particularly exciting service, John and I were relaxing and talking, when he paused and stared at me. After a long silence, he said, "Michael, why don't you come to work for me?"

"No, I can't do that."

"But you're just the man I need—"

"John, I've just been accepted to study at Fuller Seminary, and I'm going to earn a Master of Theology degree in cross-culture communication. I really want to do that. It's important for me, and I believe God wants me to go."

"You could do that part time and work for me."

"No, I don't think so."

"Think about it. Pray about it. You could learn cross-culture communication better by experience than just academics. Why, you're already doing it. Just think of the unlimited opportunities."

"There is just one problem."

"What's that?"

"It's not God's will. Elizabeth and I have prayed, and we believe that God wants me to study at Fuller."

John had the sense to know when he was licked and took it graciously. "Fine, Michael, but let's keep in close touch."

"Good idea," I said. I liked John, and the scope of his vision appealed to me.

I had no idea, however, that "close touch" meant weekly calls from John. Yet I didn't mind. It was a pleasure to hear from him so often. Later I found out that John Haggai's phone calls were renowned among his friends. When he made them, he didn't ask me to come to work for him—at least not every time. But he still wanted me, and each time that he did ask, I answered, "Maybe someday. *Now* is the time for me to study at Fuller."

In February of 1977, Elizabeth and I moved to California. By then we had two children—Sarah, 2 years old, and Natasha, 6 weeks old.

***

Then the shock came—one I had not even considered.

I showed up at the Office of Admissions at Fuller, ready to begin my studies. "Mr. Youssef, because of budgetary constraints, we just don't have the money available to give you a scholarship. Money is tight just now." As we talked, it was obvious they still wanted me to study at Fuller. "We'll help you financially the best we can."

At first I received the news as a terrible blow. *What will I do? I need the scholarship money so I can stay in the U.S. and study.* Then, as I walked from the office, I reminded myself that God had never let a lack of money stop me. He had sent me to Lebanon with nothing. Hadn't I arrived in Australia with a $500 debt and carrying borrowed funds in my pocket? God had not sent me to the United States to forsake me. He was teaching me to "trust and obey."

"It will work out," I said to myself several times. "God will provide."

How God would provide, I had no idea. I only had the assurance that I didn't have to worry about the future.

God did provide, of course. The provision came in a variety of ways. We had some savings. On occasion, churches offered me preaching opportunities. Other times, we received gifts from friends or from interested parties. Fuller Seminary helped as well. And I did end up taking a part-time job as a consultant with the Haggai Institute.

Together, Elizabeth and I faced the financial strain, and sometimes it was difficult. Often we did not know how we would pay upcoming bills. But we always paid them when they were due.

"God is faithful," I must have said almost every day. I was experiencing his faithful provision, and I knew that coming to Fuller Seminary had been the right thing to do.

\*\*\*

I loved studying at Fuller. The work was as exciting as I had envisioned. I studied hard for the next year and a half and finished my master's degree in June 1978.

Several of my professors urged me to stay on and earn a PhD in cross-culture communication. "This is obviously your field," one of them said. "And you've already shown you can do the work."

Elizabeth and I prayed about it, and it seemed right for me to enter the doctoral program. So I enrolled in the fall of 1978.

But after I started, I faced a big problem. I had already finished my first quarter and completed two basic subjects, and I was enthusiastic about the program of study. But along with the excitement came a reality that I hadn't wanted to face: we had run out of money. Our savings were exhausted. No matter how I tried to cut expenses, we were just not going to be able to continue to live in Southern California—one of the most expensive places in the U.S.—unless something happened to change the situation.

Borrowing didn't seem like the right thing to do. Being so independent (one friend called it pride), I didn't want to ask friends for help or appeal to Elizabeth's family. Both Elizabeth and I felt she needed to be home with our children instead of going back to work. We prayed for God's guidance, and the more we prayed, the more certain we felt we had taken the right stance. If God was in charge of my life, then God would have to provide. That simple thought kept me from despair.

In one of my telephone conversations with John Haggai about my studies, I mentioned that I had run out of money.

"Then why don't you come to Atlanta and work for me? I really need your help."

By then, I knew John persisted because he was led by the Lord. He felt keenly that I was the man who could help support his vision of advancing Christian leadership in the emerging third-world countries.

Yet I hesitated. *Is this God's will?* I didn't know.

As I listened to John and silently prayed, the answer suddenly seemed obvious. "Yes," I said, "this time, John, I am open if that is what the Lord wants for us."

After we hung up, I knew it was God's next step for me. Most of my heart rejoiced at this opportunity. Only one thing saddened me. Going to Atlanta, of course, meant giving up my dream for a doctoral degree in communications.

*Chapter Ten*

**Crossing Cultures**

Moving to Atlanta held a number of exciting possibilities for me. I reminded myself of John's words—I could learn about cross-culture communication by experiencing it as I traveled from country to country. As thrilling as that concept was, I still felt a longing to complete my education.

"I have surrendered to your will," I prayed. "If you still want me to have more schooling, you have to open the door."

\*\*\*

December 31, 1978, was our last day in California. We stayed the night at the Hyatt Hotel near the airport and flew to Florida the next morning. I met with John Haggai for two weeks of planning sessions. On January 18, 1979, we moved to Atlanta, and I began my work for the Haggai Institute.

It was a full-time position. Maybe even double time, although I felt right at home in what I was doing. Much of the work involved traveling around the world, and I enjoyed having the opportunity to speak to Christian leaders in dozens of countries and cultures.

In July 1980, the board voted to make me the Executive Vice President and Managing Director (a position I held until I left to start The Church of The Apostles). After that, I traveled even more. I lectured to established leaders, spoke to business people about our vision, made new contacts in a variety of countries, and built a number of long-lasting relationships.

The people I met, especially the national leaders, taught me a great deal about management and leadership. I learned from many people, but one name that loomed high was Hank McCamish, who would become one of my dearest friends. Hank was not only a friend, but I considered him one of the finest businessmen I'd ever known. He taught me to focus on my strengths and to not compare myself to others nor to criticize them. I only needed to emphasize what I had to offer and not let distractions get to me. "Don't sit on china eggs," he would say, referring to unnecessary distractions. "They never hatch."[4] I will say more about Hank in later chapters.

I loved the work, but it was also exhausting. The worst part was, because of the heavy travel schedule, I missed spending time with my family.

***

The move to California had been hard on me. I had been single during my previous moves, and that meant I had only to be concerned for myself. But I had a family when we landed in the U.S. Then our third child, Joshua, had been born in 1978, which made the move to Atlanta even harder. Joshua was six months old and needed much of Elizabeth's attention. We had one car, a borrowed one at that, for our first six months after the move.

Those first months were the hardest for my family. Despite being in the South, Atlanta was cold when we arrived—at least to us. Elizabeth and I had never lived in a cold climate. Consequently, we had no heavy clothing and no overcoats. Our kids frequently complained, "Daddy, I'm freezing." We didn't know how to keep them warm when they went outside. We

---

[4] Hank would later become Chairman of Leading The Way and also would join The Church of The Apostles.

discovered, to our amazement, that stores removed their winter clothes shortly after Christmas and put in their spring lines. We had to go from one store to another to find overcoats for all of us.

During those early months, Elizabeth suffered badly. She was home with three children, unable to leave because I was gone with the car. In California, we had lived in the seminary community. Elizabeth had people around her all the time and had the intellectual stimulation she needed. But Atlanta was different. We had come as strangers. She had to start making friends, and with three children and a lot of sickness from colds and flu, it wasn't easy. Public transportation wasn't accessible from where we lived. Eventually I had to borrow a thousand dollars to buy her a secondhand car. It improved her spirits just to be mobile.

Until we settled into a house two years later, Elizabeth was the one who suffered the most. Yet she never complained. No matter how difficult our situation, she knew it was God's will to live in Atlanta. She now not only believed in "trust and obey," she lived it.

By the time we bought the house, our finances stabilized.

\*\*\*

I loved what I was doing, but I still missed my doctoral studies. I tried not to think about it, but I couldn't forget the vision. I had surrendered my will to God, and yet the desire continued to return. Eventually, I dropped the idea; other things were more pressing. The vision of John Haggai continued to spread and more and more people joined with us in training third-world leaders. "There is no way I can ever go back to school," I said to myself several times.

Then one day a friend made a suggestion. It was one of those casual suggestions that sounded like nothing much, but it would have a profound effect on my life.

In the summer of 1980, I was talking with Dr. Jerry Beavan, who had worked with Billy Graham for many years. Jerry had been a good friend since he had visited Australia in 1976 on behalf of the Haggai Institute. "Michael, why don't you go to a secular university? Why do you have to go to a Christian school?"

That idea had never occurred to me. "I don't know," I said. "All my education has been in Christian-related schools."

"But you want to do cross-culture communication, don't you? What better place than to study in the secular world! That's crossing culture, isn't it?"

He was right. I knew it immediately. Hope was instantly rekindled.

That week I inquired at Atlanta's Emory University about admission into their PhD program. They had no degree in cross-cultural communication, but I could do the work I wanted and earn my doctoral degree in sociology of religion.

After talking it over with Elizabeth and then with John Haggai—both of whom strongly supported me—I began my doctoral studies at Emory in September 1980.

I worked full time and squeezed in the time for my studies. It was tough, and sometimes I wondered why I persisted. Many nights I fell asleep with a book in my hands. But I kept on. I was awarded my doctoral degree in 1984. It seemed to take forever. Yet I've since learned that four years is an unusually short time for someone to earn their doctorate while studying part time.

\*\*\*

Since I had been ordained as an Anglican in Australia, we naturally looked for an Episcopalian church to worship with. For our first two years, we worshipped at an Episcopal church near where we lived. However, none of the Episcopal churches we visited seemed to have the biblical orthodoxy I had witnessed in Australia. Before long, Elizabeth and I became disenchanted.

"Should we leave the Episcopal Church?" we asked each other more than once. We prayed fervently for guidance, but we never felt right about leaving. We did feel, however, that we needed to find a different congregation.

We eventually found the Cathedral of St. Philip, which was then the largest Episcopal Church in the United States. David Collins, the dean, was a Biblicist and a good speaker, and he became a good friend. We attended, enjoyed the worship, and the Cathedral soon became our church. We were content. It seemed as if God had set us up for the rest of our days. I loved my work with the Haggai Institute, we had a wonderful growing family, and we were worshiping in a church that both Elizabeth and I were comfortable in.

One day David Collins asked me to teach a Bible class. Delighted for an opportunity to teach regularly, I agreed. We had about 50 people the first time I taught. Immediately the attendance picked up. Some Sundays we had up to 150 people.

Even more important to me, I met many people who hungered for more understanding and a deeper level of commitment in their lives. Some of them had been nominal Christians. Others had come into St. Philip's as cultural Christians and had been converted to Jesus Christ through the ministry of David Collins and his wife, Jenny. Now I had the opportunity to feed them and help them in their growth.

As I prepared to teach each week, I prayed and hoped they would receive help and encouragement. I felt as if the class had been made just for me to teach; it fulfilled my need to be involved with the congregation and to make a difference. The Sunday school hour was a high point of my week.

During the years we worshiped at the Cathedral and I taught the class, I continued to travel and work for Haggai. My work at the Cathedral was done strictly as a volunteer; I took no money. It was my way of serving, and I never stopped being thankful for the opportunity they gave me to open the Bible and to speak from God's Word.

I had no way of knowing that our worship at St. Philip's was not the end of the journey. It was only the next step.

The real vision was almost ready to unfold.

*Chapter Eleven*

**Restless Vision**

*Restless* is the word I would have used to describe myself in 1984. I would have also added: exhausted, overworked, involved, and excited. But I had never experienced the inner restlessness before. Maybe it was because I had worked double-duty to finish my doctoral degree, and now I didn't have any place to re-channel my energies. At least, that's what I told myself.

But there was more to it than that. Life was going well for me. On every front, I was having the best time of my life. The work at the Haggai Institute continued to expand. Not only had we adjusted to Atlanta, but the city had become home. We had many fine friends; our children were involved in school activities, our fourth child, Jonathan, had been born; I published my first book through Thomas Nelson Publishers; and I taught a class at St. Philip's and even preached from time to time.

It should have been enough.

But it wasn't.

Something was gnawing at me, but I didn't know what it was. *What's wrong*, I asked myself.

Finally I realized that God had been trying to speak to me and I hadn't been listening. I was too busy doing God's work to hear anything new. Many of us can get so bogged down in the mechanics of ministry that we cease to hear God. Once I knew where to seek the answer, I learned the cause of my restlessness. I began to listen to God, and then the message came through.

Finally I voiced it to Elizabeth, "I need to get into a consistent preaching ministry." I wasn't exactly sure what I was saying, but the general idea was clear. "I don't feel any great desire to be a pastor," I said, "but I do need to have an ongoing, consistent place to preach the gospel." Frankly, I didn't want the pastoral responsibilities. I knew only that a desire was growing in me to be more fully related to a congregation, and I had to do something about it. It was time, yet again, to trust and obey.

Elizabeth understood and stood with me. Perhaps she had been aware of the disquiet within me longer than I had.

During the period when I was beginning to listen to God, David Collins announced his retirement as dean—the presiding official at a cathedral.

His retirement was sad news for me. Not only did I respect him and count him a friend, I was afraid his replacement would not have the same biblical commitment.

I tried not to worry about the future of St. Philip's. During that time, I still taught my Sunday school class, and I loved the people who studied with me week after week. There was a lot to feel good about. When David announced his retirement, people did talk to me. Since I was an ordained minister and they liked me, it was only natural for some of them to suggest I succeed David.

I listened to them and said, "I don't think this is God's will. But you pray, and I'll pray for guidance." It was flattering that they had that level of confidence in my ministry and wanted me as their rector. But it was not what God wanted for me—no matter how often I prayed, it just didn't feel right. All I could do was to encourage them to pray for God to provide us with the right person.

A number of people contacted Judson Child, the Bishop of the Diocese of Atlanta, to suggest my name as the new dean at St. Phillip's. He didn't think that was right for me, either.

One day we had lunch together and he said, lovingly and honestly, "Michael, you're an evangelist. Right now the cathedral needs healing. I don't think you're the person who can placate the various factions." He really meant that they needed a compromiser—and I was not one.

"I agree," I said. As I saw it, the congregation had divided into five theological camps, and David Collins was one of those rare individuals who could keep the factions together and still be faithful to the gospel. I just wasn't a man who could placate those who openly stated, "We don't want all this Jesus stuff." Because of my strong commitment to biblical principles, I wasn't good at that style of leadership within the church.

I had also become increasingly aware that I was a man with a strong personality. If I was the leader, I had to lead. I would work with anyone who wanted to follow, but I was just as ready to say, "If you can't follow my leadership style, I invite you to get out of the way." A weakness perhaps, but it was also a strength.

As a leader, I believed I was both the engineer and conductor of the train. I tried to be gentle about that, but I only wanted those on board who wanted to be there and who wanted to go where the train was headed. I didn't want to force anyone to go along for the ride, only to discover they were traveling in a different direction than they wanted to go.

One day at a breakfast in his house, Bishop Child asked me, "What is it you feel led to do?"

Suddenly I knew. "To plant a new church."

"Why?"

"Because I don't think I could fit into a church that is already established. It would already have its own tradition and its own style of worship. I'd have to start all over to have the comfort level that I want. So if I had to do that, wouldn't it be better to start with a new place?"

"You may be exactly right."

Bishop Child and I talked together for a few more minutes, but I could hardly wait to leave. Something was bubbling inside my heart. Until the moment I spoke the words to him, I had not understood what I wanted to do—what I really wanted to do. That restlessness had been stirred up, but I didn't know the direction to go. Now I knew. It seemed so obvious. My own words had given me the guidance I needed.

How could I go about starting an Episcopal church? Where would I begin? When was the right time? How could I maintain my heavy work load at the Haggai Institute and still find time to start a church? Would it mean leaving my position with the Institute? Although my joy and excitement never left, now I was filled with a different kind of unrest.

But at least I knew the direction.

Now I had to wait for the full vision to unfold.

## Chapter Twelve

## A New Step

Bill Bugg was a friend of mine, and we had met for lunch to discuss some business matters. But just before we got ready to leave, Bill said, "You know, Michael, I've been concerned about you. Is there something wrong?"

"You're concerned about me, really?"

"You don't seem contented. I don't know what it is, but it bothers me. You're restless, aren't you? You're not your usual self."

"No, I'm not. And it's odd that you use the word restless. That's exactly the way I've been feeling."

"What is God saying to you?"

"Plant an evangelical church," I blurted out and then immediately regretted it. I didn't feel ready to say anything publicly about the vision.

Bill's eyes lit up. "What are you doing to make that happen?"

"I'm praying about it. Right now I'm only in the praying stage. I don't want to do anything until I'm sure about what to do. It isn't time."

"This sounds wonderful. You need to get down to business and do something. Don't you think you need to move on it?"

"Just as soon as God guides me." Those weren't defensive words, but I knew I couldn't do anything until the Holy Spirit directed me.

"I'll pray with you for guidance."

For the next few weeks, nothing became clearer. Daily I prayed for guidance. I was willing to wait—at least I knew there was something on the horizon. But I still struggled in my spirit. I didn't want to miss God's will, and there were also earthly things to consider. I had a job with the best working conditions. In everything I did or suggested, John Haggai showed unqualified support and cooperation. I was traveling around the world. I had just published my book, *The Leadership Style of Jesus*, with Victor Books. Although released by a small Christian publisher, the book was doing well. My family was happy, and we had many friends at the Cathedral. To leave all that to start a new church would be crazy—unless it was God's utmost plan.

What about my family? What if I started a new church and it failed? How would I provide for my family? I wanted to trust and obey. It wasn't that I was afraid, but I believed as a Christian and as a steward that I had to think carefully about the cost and the possibility of failure.

Although I didn't yet have a strong direction from God, I knew I was getting closer to making important decisions.

\*\*\*

During the next few weeks, Bill and I talked several times about a new church. He would ask, "Anything?" and I would say that I was still talking to God and waiting for guidance.

Then one day, Bill said, "I think it's time to do something. I've set up a luncheon meeting with three other men. They need to hear what you have to say."

At first I waffled, but Bill insisted. "Unless you start talking about it, you won't start working at it."

"Okay," I said and laughed. "I'll be there."

In the fall of 1986 the five of us met at the Capital City Club in downtown Atlanta. The three he invited were good friends from the Cathedral—John Minor, Gene Hall, and Andy Huber. Bill hosted the meeting. Briefly he told them about our previous conversations, and then he turned to me and said, "Share your vision with them."

Reluctantly I told them about the tug I felt to start an evangelical Episcopal church. Specifically, I had been thinking that one was needed in the Buckhead/Vinings area of Atlanta. "I know God wants me to move in this direction, but I'm resistant to do it right now. I'm not sure it's God's time."

"Nothing has to be done right now," Gene said, "and we won't do anything either unless you want our help."

"We are here to help you," said John, "because we're your friends, and we want to support you."

After thanking them for their interest, I said, "I've got to pray and let God do the deciding. I don't want to make a mistake and do the wrong thing or act prematurely."

For perhaps forty-five minutes we discussed the idea of starting a new church. These were good men. They would be straight with me, no matter how much it might hurt me to hear their opinions. After I told them everything, I asked, "What do you think? Give me your honest opinion."

"It's not going to work." Gene spoke first. "It's impossible. Michael, it just won't work."

"Why won't it?" I asked.

"For one thing, it will never work for an Egyptian to move into Buckhead and start a church with just nothing. For another, the

Bishop will never allow it. I am the chair of the stewardship committee at the Cathedral and they would be worried you will siphon the Evangelical's money – which is the majority of it."

I couldn't argue with a single thing he said.

"What is your gift, Michael?" asked Andy.

"Preaching and teaching," I said without hesitation.

He shook his head. "I really don't think so. I don't think you're a good preacher.

You're one of the best teachers around, but you're not a preacher. So I don't think it will work either."

Andy's words stung, but I knew they came from his heart. And as I later reminded myself, I had asked each man to speak frankly.

"I believe you hear from the Lord," John said. "You are a man of God. I have confidence that whatever the Lord tells you to do, you will obey him."

Other things were said, but I can't remember most of them. These were friends. I know they said nothing in unkindness, but spoke out of genuine concern for me and for the work of God.

Yet as I drove back to my office, I felt wounded, hurt, kicked, and knocked around. Their words had stung deeply. I had shared my excitement about a church, and they gave me all the reasons why it wouldn't work. No one likes to be told that his ideas are unworkable. As I would realize later, their words hurt because starting a church was becoming increasingly important to me. Without knowing it, I was seeking affirmation from my friends. When they didn't give me that encouragement, my spirits plunged.

But as I continued to drive, I slowly pulled out of my self-pity. I began to feel somewhat relieved. Even though I had spoken to my friends reluctantly, they had listened carefully and given me honest feedback. Maybe they had saved me from not following God's will.

"Lord, I believe in the confirmation of the saints. If you speak to me, you will confirm it through your people. Obviously, you are not giving me the green light to go ahead. I'm going to believe that this is your message to stay where I am and to forget the idea."

I began to feel calm. I had made my best presentation, and those caring men had told me I was going in the wrong direction. Obviously, to start a church was not what God wanted.

"God, I'm waiting. I'm waiting and I know you'll show me your will."

*"You are foolish."*

Those three words rang through my mind, disturbing my calmness. God was speaking to me, not in an audible voice, but so distinctly through my thoughts that I had no doubt it was Him.

"What do you mean?"

*"You are foolish for telling those people. You didn't pray about whether you ought to go and share your vision. You didn't get guidance from me first."*

"Forgive me."

*"You are foolish to listen to others and not to listen to me."*

By then I felt very troubled. They had expressed their opinions and, on the whole, they told me the idea was unworkable. Instead of turning to God, I had allowed their responses to guide me. I asked God's forgiveness again.

*"You were foolish, Michael, but I am going to overrule."* Then the Lord reminded me of my own motto: trust and obey. Those men spoke from their hearts, but they were not prepared. They hadn't prayed. They were expressing their opinions only.

"Okay, God," I said, "I'm back to square one."

For the last few minutes of the ride, I had peace.

God had spoken.

*Chapter Thirteen*

**Stepping Forward**

After the luncheon where I presented my vision for a church, I drove back to the Haggai Institute, perhaps half-an-hour's drive. When I arrived at the office, I already had a message that Bill Bugg had called. Immediately I returned his call.

"I was disappointed by the outcome of the meeting," he said. "I'd been so excited about starting a new church, and I assumed the others would catch the excitement. I know you're disappointed, too."

"Yes, I am." Then I told Bill about my experience while driving back to the office.

"Let's have another meeting! When they hear that—"

"No more meetings. Not now anyway. Right now I'm going to spend time praying about it."

"May I call you a week from now?"

"Sure, why not?" I laughed. Bill was persistent. "By then, I believe I'll have a stronger sense of direction."

Exactly seven days later, Bill called. "Michael, I've been praying. I believe a new church is God's will. I've also talked again to the three men, and we'd like to have another meeting with you."

"All right," I said. Before we set the meeting, I told him, "Since we last spoke, I've been active. I've written to Bishop Child formally asking to start a mission church."

"Oh, really?" From his response, I felt Bill's excitement building.

A few days later, Bill arranged a second meeting at Gene Hall's office. Bill Bugg invited two more friends from St. Philip's, David Coker and Tom Hall, and I asked Victor Oliver to go with me. Victor was a senior editor at Thomas Nelson Publishers and also a close friend. I brought him because of how disappointed I had felt after the previous meeting. I needed someone to give me emotional support.

The second time I shared my vision with them, I did it without hesitancy. I knew what God had laid on my heart. This time the vision was clear. I told them what I wanted to do and how I planned to do it. For instance, I believed we needed to raise enough money so that we would not have to ask the Diocese of Atlanta for funds. Also, I had already asked several people where we needed an Episcopal church. "One answer kept coming back: the Vinings area." All of us knew that Vinings was a growing area on the northwest side of Atlanta.

After I said everything on my heart, the debate started.

"I really don't like your leaving the Cathedral," David Coker said. "You're preaching the gospel. If you leave, we will lose your strong voice. I'm biased, of course, in telling you it's not a good idea."

I listened as each man spoke, honestly sharing from their hearts.

"Michael, you're a strong person, and you know what you want," one of them said, "so you might as well tell us everything you plan to do. I really want to know, and then I can decide if it's a good plan and if I can help."

"I'll only do what the Lord wants," I said. That may have sounded simplistic and pious, but that was exactly how I felt. If we couldn't do it God's way, I didn't want any part of it.

Victor Oliver, although not previously known by everyone, finally spoke up. He became quite vocal that our diocese needed an evangelical church. I especially remember one statement he made. "If God has laid this on Michael's heart, then we need to support him."

After more discussion, I finally said, "Each of you wants to know God's will for yourself, and you desire what's best for me. I've heard everything you have to say. I've written to the Bishop. Here's how I would like to leave this matter. If he says yes, we accept that as divine guidance."

"Sounds like a good way to test the Lord's direction," someone said.

The others agreed. We ended our meeting with prayer.

***

That meeting took place late in 1986. By January of 1987, Bishop Child had not responded. Finally I sent him a second letter with a copy of the original. In essence, I said, "Please give me an answer of yes or no. I just want to know."

Two days later, he called me and we had breakfast together at his house. He said, "I'm referring your request to the Department of Congregations and Development. You can meet with them." It was obvious that he didn't oppose my idea.

During our conversation, he suggested we name the new church—if we started one—The Church of The Apostles.

"Good name," I said. "It makes me feel like we'd be moving in the tradition of the apostles."

Bishop Child asked me to write an official letter to him, which he would give to Herschel Atkinson, his liaison. Herschel would take the letter to the committee, which was responsible for starting new churches.

A few days later, the committee invited me to a meeting. I spent quite some time explaining my vision. When I paused, a Jamaican clergyman by the name of Don Taylor, who later became a bishop in the Virgin Islands, said, "Let's cut through this and get down to the basics. Our committee hasn't met in a long time, so we have to get ourselves rolling again. There are two questions we have to answer. Number one, does the Bishop want this church?"

"The Bishop said he wanted the committee to explore it," answered Herschel Atkinson.

"Okay," Don said. "That's certainly not a negative answer anyway. Can we assume that he is at least not opposed?" He waited and the others nodded. "Now, let's get to the second question. How much money is this going to cost the Diocese?"

"Nothing," I said.

Every member of the committee stared at me. That just wasn't the way Episcopalians started new churches. The Diocese always had to make a heavy financial commitment to support a founding rector, rent space, and buy property.

When I said, "Nothing," I knew that was an audacious statement. In my praying and agonizing over the new church, God had spoken to me that we would not need to ask the Diocese for money. I had no idea how it would work or where the funds would come from, but I did know that God had spoken to me.

"If you approve of my starting a new church," I said, shifting my gaze from member to member, "it will not cost you anything. We only want you to grant us permission."

"We're wasting our time then," Don said. "We have the opportunity to start a new church near Vinings, and it won't cost us anything. I can't think of anything more exciting. I'm ready to vote."

The committee voted. They gave us unanimous approval.

After they voted, a thought struck me. "Wait a minute. Your approval is fine, but don't we need to check with the neighboring parishes?"

"That's correct," said Don. "If this project does not cost the Diocese anything, and if none of the neighborhood parishes object, then we are totally behind this."

***

Immediately I began to contact the rectors of the congregations that would be affected if we started a church in Vinings. Shortly after that, Herschel called for a meeting with the rectors of Episcopal churches on Atlanta's north side. We met at St. Anne's, an established church in the northwest section of Atlanta.

Also attending the meeting was Frank Allan, rector of St. Anne's, who had recently been voted as the Bishop Cojudicator (the person who automatically takes over when the bishop of the diocese retires or becomes incompetent to do his duties). The deans of the North Atlanta and Marietta convocations also attended. Rectors of local congregations had been invited, but most of them sent messages that said, "We have no objection."

It was a long but necessary meeting. Frank Allan and his assistant, Roger Ard, showed sincere support. One man voiced opposition—a surprise to me. It came from a good friend, David Dye. He was unhappy with the diocese and spent time laying out his complaints. Finally, he said, "This isn't really in opposition to you, Michael, or to the request for a new church. This is a much more basic opposition to other issues."

After some discussion, David said, "As far as starting this new church, I have no objections." (Incidentally, David later became a Roman Catholic priest.)

The consensus from those gathered was that they would not hinder us and we could move ahead.

By then, our small group of prayer partners and I were no longer referring to this as the "new church." We began to use our name, The Church of The Apostles. That was an unconscious but important step. We were taking on an identity.

***

One of the first decisions to make was where to meet initially for services. Eventually we would have to buy land, but that wasn't a practical possibility in the first stages of the church. Elizabeth suggested we rent the chapel at Lovett School.

The Lovett School, a beautiful, prestigious, private school on the north side of Atlanta, seemed like the ideal place. Their chapel seated six hundred. I sincerely believed that if God was in this venture, we would fill all those seats within a few months. "Let's see if they'll let us rent it," I said.

By December 1986, plans were moving ahead. The small group of men who had been with me from the beginning stayed with me, but I worked alone on the practical details of starting The Church of The Apostles.

Word spread. Episcopalians around metro Atlanta heard of our new venture. Even non-Episcopalians showed excitement. One Christian brother said, "I know it takes money. Here's the first contribution." The check was for $10,000, and the man, a Presbyterian, later became part of our congregation. He gave simply because of our friendship.

The next day another friend gave me a check for $5,000. Then several other individuals gave us unsolicited offerings to help us get started.

Now we had a name, and we had enough money to open a bank account, which we did as a designated fund within the Diocese. Those were small things in some ways, but each step encouraged us and confirmed we were moving a little closer to starting worship services.

For a few weeks, euphoric feelings overwhelmed me. *It's happening. A church—starting right from the beginning, with no tradition, no inherited theological issues. Just exactly what fits my personality.*

Then I made another mistake. I got expert advice, and I listened to it without consulting God.

That simple mistake could have ruined everything. If God had not intervened once again, The Church of The Apostles would not exist today.

*Chapter Fourteen*

## An Intervening Voice

"When will you start your worship services?"

That was the most frequent question I heard from friends. They knew it took time, but many were excited to see us get moving. Frankly, the question pleased me. I perceived interest, openness, and spiritual support from those who asked.

"September," I answered, "early in September." I was saying that in January of 1987. Eight months didn't seem like such a long time with all the things we needed to do. And yet, my heart was aching to get going.

Why September instead of June or April? As part of my homework, I read and studied everything I could on church growth. I spoke with the Bishop and with anyone else who seemed to know anything about starting new churches. Informally, I consulted with some of the best church-planting strategists in the nation. One well-known strategist said, "Never start a church in the spring. Even worse is to try to start one in the middle of summer. If you're smart, you'll wait until after school begins, after the first of September."

He (and others) pointed out the facts of life about churches. People travel on vacation during the summer. Attendance plummets. Church giving dips from June through August. "But come September," one respected expert told me, "people are ready to get back into their routines. That's the perfect time for any new program or for starting a church."

Without praying, without thinking about it more, I accepted their word. After all, experts knew what they were doing. That's why they were the experts.

I also had a heavy travel schedule lined up for the Haggai Institute. Some of the travel would take me overseas on weekends during August. So I didn't want to start a church if I couldn't be there every Sunday myself.

"That's such a long way off," some people said when I mentioned September, but that was the worst response I got. No one actually disagreed, especially when I explained the reason. "Makes sense," they would say, even though they continued to want to start sooner.

***

In January 1987, Elizabeth and I met with Al Cash, the headmaster at The Lovett School. We had already planned to enroll both Sarah and Natasha there. We told Al we wanted to rent The Lovett School chapel as our initial starting place.

"Who are your members? How many do you have?"

"We have six, at least for now. All of them are members of the Youssef family."

He looked quizzically at me. "You don't even have members other than your family and you want to rent our chapel?"

"That's right."

"Have you seen the size of our chapel? It seats six hundred."

"That will be all right for a start," I said. My words probably blew his mind, but I *knew* God was going to bless us immensely and that our attendance would grow right from the beginning.

"This doesn't make a lot of sense," he said. "Wouldn't it be wiser to start with a smaller place and then—"

"People will come if we have a place to worship." I knew that much. "And why should you have to worry about how many people we have?"

"You're right, of course," he said. "But for so few—"

"We'll have many, many people," I said. "In fact, I hope your chapel won't be too small." I was laughing then, but I was also serious. I knew that God was calling us to start The Church of The Apostles. I also knew that even after all the struggles to get approval (and there would be other problems ahead), I had a definite assurance that God was going to do something beyond our expectations.

Al listened for several minutes as I shared my vision. "I know this is God leading us," I said.

By the time I finished, Al enthusiastically supported the idea. "Here's what you need to do. Write a letter to me asking for permission to use our facilities. Once I get the letter, I'll take it to our board, and then we'll let you know."

For the next few weeks I negotiated with the board at The Lovett School. At first, they were hesitant to lease us the facilities because they had never done anything like that before. So far as I am aware, no one opposed the idea of leasing us space, but they were just being cautious.

On March 21, 1987, I met with Al Cash, the senior staff members of Lovett, and the two attorneys involved in the negotiation. I assured them that we would take care of the building, and they could dispossess us if we ever became unruly or if they had complaints about anything. We assured them that we would hire janitors to clean after we left the building.

The representatives of Lovett were kind and friendly. They were enthusiastic and assured me that they would take the matter to the full board for a vote on April 29. They felt confident that the others would agree for us to use the chapel starting the first of September. We only needed to work out the details.

***

Although I make a lot of mistakes as a human being and certainly as a leader, the one thing that gives me confidence is that God knows my heart. More than anything, I want God's will for me, for my family, and for those who accept my leadership. Because of that, I know God overrules me when I start heading the wrong way.

And I was making a wrong move.

The corrective message came from the Lord through a man whom I considered an acquaintance, Gil Meredith. We had met briefly at the Cathedral on a few occasions. In March, I received a letter from him. He hadn't known how to get hold of me, but he contacted a friend of mine who gave him my address.

Although I didn't save the letter, the message went something like this: "I am really led by the Lord to say that you should start your church earlier than September. I don't know the reason, only that it is important for you to start sooner."

Immediately I wrote back saying, "Thank you for your interest and concern. We have set early September for our beginning date."

To my shame, I didn't even pray about his message. Why should I? My path seemed clear. It was, after all, the practical thing to do. If I tried to start earlier, it would have messed up my travel plans and gotten the church off to a bad start. I did not see any need to pray about it.

A month later, on Wednesday morning, April 29, 1987, I was at Gene Hall's house. Both Gene and I had worshiped at St.

Philip's three days earlier, which was Easter Sunday. Both of us had left saddened and unhappy. For me, it was the most joyless sermon I had ever heard on Easter. As I left church that Sunday, I wondered how long I could keep listening to messages that affected me that way. *God, help me not to be critical but to wait patiently for you to take me out of here.*

On the Wednesday after Easter, Gene and I were on our knees praying together about matters not related to the new church. The bell rang and Gene went to answer. When he came back, Andy Huber and Gil Meredith were following him into the room.

"Called your office," Andy said. "We told them it was imperative that we get in touch with you this morning. That's how we knew where you were."

"Must be really important for you to track me down," I said.

"They said you were leaving for Dallas this afternoon. Otherwise we could have waited until tomorrow."

We sat down, and after an awkward silence, Andy said, "Gil has something to say to you." Andy leaned forward and stared at me intently, "You need to listen to him, Michael."

"Sure," I said.

"You don't know me very well," Gil said. He was a gentle, soft-spoken man, and I sensed it wasn't easy for him to tell me what he needed to say. "Ever since I heard about the new church, I've been happy and excited for you. I've prayed for the success of the church, and I believe it's of the Lord."

I smiled, glad that he hadn't come to try to convince me not to move forward. And, frankly, I had forgotten about the letter he had written to me in March.

"You see, Michael, God has spoken to me about the church. Not just once, but several times. I wrote you a letter—"

"Oh, yes," I said. Only then did I remember.

87

"God just won't give me any rest from this," he said. "I am to tell you that you must start the church earlier. I don't have any kind of date for you, but it has to be before September."

"Gil, I appreciate your concern, and thank you for praying, but it's impossible. I can't do it any earlier than September. It's that simple."

"I know God has spoken to me," Gil said. He was still soft-spoken, but his words came with such conviction that I couldn't ignore what he said.

"Why don't we pray, Michael?" Gene suggested. "Why don't we see what the Lord tells you and us?"

"Yes," I said, "that's the only way to get this clear, isn't it?"

The four of us knelt on our knees in Gene's den and prayed. Andy started, "God, speak to us. Give us wisdom."

While we were on our knees, God did speak. He spoke quietly, but definitely. In a matter of minutes, I received an inner certainty that Gil was right and I was wrong. After our united prayer, I said, "Gil, you're right. We're going to start the new church just as soon as possible. I'm sorry I allowed my own thoughts and schedule to drive me and not hear His voice."

"I know it's right," Gene said. "I don't understand why, but it is."

"This *is* a word from the Lord," Andy added.

Right then we made three important decisions. As we would see in the days ahead, those decisions were far more important than any of us realized. First, we agreed to open our own bank account that very day in the name of The Church of The Apostles.

Second, Gil volunteered, and we agreed, that he should call the Stouffer Waverly Hotel and reserve a conference room for every Sunday through August

Third, we set the date for our first service—it would be May 10, Mother's Day. That was less than two weeks away.

When we made that third decision, logic said we were committing suicide. Who starts a church on the day when people go to church to honor their mothers? But we had listened to Gil, we had prayed, and each of us felt we had heard God speak.

"Doesn't God have a wonderful sense of humor?" one of them said as we left each other.

Yes, I thought, and God is so kind to correct me when I walk in the wrong direction.

*Chapter Fifteen*

## Opposition

Our decision was made. We were going to start The Church of The Apostles in two weeks. When I left Atlanta for Dallas the next morning, I could hardly contain my joy. Once again God had proven faithful.

By the time I arrived in Dallas, however, I had a call waiting for me from my office back in Atlanta. My administrative assistant said, "Bishop Allan called. He says it's urgent for you to get in touch with him today."

After she gave me my other messages, I called Bishop Allan.

"I need to see you, Michael. Just as soon as possible."

"I'm returning tomorrow afternoon," I said, "but can't it wait until Monday?" The next day was Friday, and I wouldn't land back in Atlanta until 3:00.

"No, it's too urgent."

"Okay," I said. "I can be at your office tomorrow afternoon by 4:00." Naturally, I wanted to know what was so urgent, but I sensed it would be better to discuss whatever it was face to face.

"I'll wait for you," he said.

Friday afternoon, I drove directly from the airport to meet with him. When I arrived at the Diocese offices, I immediately noticed that the usual cars were not in the parking lot. Everyone had left early. As I walked inside, I had a gut feeling that someone was going to try to do a hatchet job. In that very instant, deep inside my heart, I knew that Bishop Allan wanted to undo the decision to start The Church of The Apostles. Maybe I figured that out myself. Maybe it was God speaking and preparing me as I made my way to the Bishop's office. But regardless of where that knowledge came from, I knew it was right.

Once I reached his office, my suspicion was instantly confirmed when I saw the Bishop's face.

"Have a seat. I want to talk to you." The tension in his voice told me this was not going to be pleasant for either of us. He went to the corner of his office and retrieved a large map of metropolitan Atlanta.

"It's just this, Michael. If you start a church in the Vinings area, it's too close to St. Anne's and it's too close to the Cathedral." Vinings, as both of us knew from our previous discussions, was two and a half miles from St. Anne's and five miles from the Cathedral. "You need to think about moving the church to some other place."

Frankly, I was weary with talking about the issue, but I knew I had to defend the new church development. By then, I had figured out the real reason for his calling me. "Bishop," I said, trying to sound respectful, "we have gone around and around on this many times. It's just too late. We're already moving ahead."

"The truth is, Michael, we don't really need an Episcopal church in the Vinings area." He pointed to the map again. "Please listen carefully to me. I've called you because there's a major concern on the part of the Cathedral—"

"But I understood they were in favor of this."

"They've been rethinking it. Apparently, some of them are concerned they will lose the fundamentalists from their church."

That was the real reason. I had not made any attempt to get any of those he called "fundamentalists" to follow me to the new location, but in fact, many of them had supported me. I had gone out of my way to discourage them from coming. I didn't want to be accused of trying to pull members from the Cathedral or anywhere else. I wasn't interested in doing that. But perhaps more important than the people, it was no secret that the so-called "fundamentalists" were the heaviest financial givers at the Cathedral.

"I don't like being categorized as a 'fundamentalist,'" I said. "I'm not objecting to being recognized as both conservative and evangelical, but I just don't like labels." In his mind, and in the minds of other clergy, believing the Bible as the Word of God and in the divinity of Jesus Christ made me a "fundamentalist."

"Regardless," he said, "you and I both know the people I'm talking about. The Cathedral is very, very concerned." He mentioned names of several prominent members and generous contributors who were likely to go to Apostles.

"I haven't asked any of them to join us—"

"But they will."

"That's their decision to make, then, isn't it?"

The discussion went on until one of us said that if certain individuals left St. Philip's, it would drastically decrease the Cathedral's resources. "Resources" was a safe word for money.

"That's the concern, isn't it?" I asked. "If they leave, so does their money."

"As a matter fact, I got a call yesterday morning from the senior warden. He expressed a great concern about just that problem."

I said I would contact him. He was a man I knew and liked, and he was also CEO of one of the city's larger banks.

"It's not only the money," the Bishop said. "Just as important is the mix and diversity of people that the Cathedral wants to preserve. The Cathedral should be the place of worship for every kind of Episcopalian, regardless of theology."

"Bishop, I understand your concern," I said, pausing to choose my words carefully. I wanted to show my respect for his office, but I would not back down. "You see, we already have official permission to start a new church. We are going to start our church." Before he could continue with further arguments, I asked, "Will you try to put any limits on us?"

"What kind of limits?"

"By saying that we can't receive members from churches that are within a certain radius," I said. "You can do that if you want. Our purpose is not to rob other congregations. Our concern is to be an evangelistic congregation. We want to reach nominal Christians and the uncommitted."

The Bishop wasn't seeing the new church the same way I did. He was thinking in terms of a local parish, but I knew that God was raising a regional church with a global vision.

"You don't have to worry about limitations." He explained that could not happen because the church's canon law prevented rectors from objecting to lay people moving their letter of membership.

"Wait a minute." Bishop Allan turned to the map again. "Look at this, Michael. If you're intent on starting a new church, think about this. Several people have talked with me. We've been looking at the map and trying to see where we really do need a church. The truth is we don't need one in Vinings. Here's where we do need to start an Episcopal church." He pointed to a spot on the map. From where I was standing, I couldn't tell where he was pointing, but it seemed to me that it was near the Georgia-North

Carolina border. "Right there," he pointed again. "That's where we badly need an Episcopal presence."

As I looked, I realized that would put it in a rural mountainous area. Exactly where I would feel hopelessly out of place. "Sorry," I said, "but it's too late. We've already been organized."

"You have? Already? How is that possible?"

"We've opened our own bank account. We have a function room booked for the summer months at the Waverly. And we've negotiated a contract to use the chapel at Lovett School beginning in September. As a matter of fact, I've had several night meetings with their board. We've signed a legal contract."

The color left his face. "I thought you weren't starting until September."

"That was the way I had planned it. But recently I met with a group of the men who are helping me with the planning. They felt we needed to start early, right away. So that's exactly what we're doing."

"Please understand that it's not my idea to delay your starting. I'm just responding to the concerns of several individuals from the Cathedral."

"I understand."

He stared at me for several seconds. I think he realized he could not stop us. "Two things I want to tell you, however," he said. "First, I don't like your meeting at Lovett—"

"Too late. It's already legally signed—"

"And, second, we expect ten percent of your income to come to the Diocese."

"You don't need to worry about that," I said. "We will do the right thing."

"Another thing," he said, "we would like to have a monthly report of the work, as well as a monthly financial statement."

"No objection whatsoever," I said. "You aren't questioning our right to have our own bank account, are you?"

"Oh, no. If you like, you can use the Diocese tax-exempt number for now."

Once our positions were clear, the Bishop then spoke to me about the various legal and ecclesiastical steps we needed to take to start a new church, and I was grateful. I expressed my willingness to cooperate and was genuinely pleased that he would help us. I appreciated also that he would advise me on learning the mechanics of the parish. That was new territory for me, of course, so I welcomed all the advice I could get. And in my heart, I had decided that I would pray before acting on anyone's advice.

We ended the meeting on a warm, cordial note.

***

Later, I met with the senior warden of the Cathedral for lunch at the World Trade Club. He was quite open about his concern. "I'm afraid that a new church will siphon the moneyed people from St. Philip's and that will harm the Cathedral." He also urged me to delay getting started.

"Look," I said, "I have not asked one person from the Cathedral to come to our church. Not one. Even the four men who are helping me have not committed themselves to move their membership. The people who are doing the most for me right now are doing so because they want to help. That's all. They are not committing themselves to stay with me. Gene Hall, for instance, has no plans to move his membership."[5]

"Is that so?"

---

[5] Gene Hall did not make his decision to leave the Cathedral until July. At that time, he told the dean himself, "I'm going to go with Michael." Gene wanted to be up front about his intentions, but he also promised that he would give a certain dollar amount to the Cathedral to show his continued support for the Cathedral and his interest there.

"I'm telling you, it's so. Not Bill Bugg, either. Bill said that he and his wife would not leave unless God calls them to do so. I don't think he's had a change of heart," I said. "I don't want to pull members from the Cathedral or from St. Anne's or any other place. I don't want to take people with me. I want to reach people who are not committed."

He kept insisting that people would leave, regardless of my noble intentions. Even those who didn't leave, he believed, would divert part of their contributions to the new work.

"I don't believe in building at the expense of someone else," I said. "And I'd be happy to make a public statement that urges members of St. Philip's not to join us."

We parted amicably, and again I tried to reassure him.

His final words were, "You may be right, but I'm still worried."

***

Earlier in the year I had talked about the new church with John Sanders, the new dean at St. Philip's. John was initially supportive. However, later he would explain that because he was new to the city, he had not realized the close proximity of Vinings to the Cathedral.

I decided I needed to have another meeting with John. Despite having met with him earlier, I felt I needed to reassure him that I wasn't trying to "siphon off" people or money.

We met for lunch, and I told him, "I want you to know from me exactly what is happening, and how far we've gone in preparing for Apostles."

During our conversation, I mentioned one man who had said that he and his wife were joining us. "I didn't ask or invite them, please understand that."

"Oh, I understand. There will be several families. That's only natural."

Theologically, we were worlds apart, but I liked John a great deal, and I didn't want to do anything to sabotage his work. I tried to assure him that I would not intentionally or knowingly do anything to hinder his ministry at St. Philip's. He said he understood, and he thanked me for being sensitive to his feelings. We parted on an upbeat, friendly basis.

As I drove home, I prayed, "God, help us to go about this honorably. Help us to be above reproach in every step we take."

I had done everything I knew how to do.

I felt at peace.

*Chapter Sixteen*

## The Doors Open

Sunday, May 10, 1987, was Mother's Day.

Sunday, May 10, 1987, was the birthday of The Church of The Apostles.

We worshipped on the second floor of the Waverly Hotel in the Hallmark Room, which was one of their function rooms. Our service began at 9:00. We had asked for a setup of fifty chairs. And in true Episcopal tradition, we had agreed that we would offer communion every Sunday.

No ads had been taken out. No big announcements. Anyone who came would do so because they had received a word-of-mouth invitation.

I had hoped we would have at least twenty-five people. "But five or fifty, we are starting. I know it's God's time and we're doing it God's way."

Fifty-two people attended that first worship service, thirty-one of them adults.[6]

---

[6] Of the four men who started with me at the beginning, Gene Hall and Bill Bugg are members, John Miner remained at the Cathedral, and Andy Huber was with us for three years. Andy later left to lead a mission downtown for the mentally handicapped.

## ORDER OF WORSHIP

```
May 10, 1987 (Mother's Day) was first meeting of
The Church of The Apostles.

It met at 9AM in the Hallmark Room at the Wavery
Hotel.

Service consisted of:

Psalm:  23 by Gil Meredith
Epistle:  I Peter 2:19-25 by Andy Huber
Gospel:  John 10:1-10 by Michael Youssef
Prayers of the People:  Gene Hall
Sermon:  Michael Youssef
Sermon Text:  Isaiah 49:14-16


Songs:  Our God Reigns
        All Hail the Power of Jesus Name
        For God So Loved
```

In attendance were:

Fran Beaver and children: Hannah, Courrie, Elizsabeth, and Howell

Bill and Nine Bugg

Bill and Eleanor Cheney

Marcus and Mary Ellen Cook

Gene and Joan Hall

Andy and Frances Huber and teens: Tim and Robbie

Gerald and Lannie Lambert and children: Lachlan and Jean

Bud and Marge Lindsey (Bakersfield, CA – old friends who were staying at the hotel)

Fred and Betty Lines and children: Alex, Michael, Hudson, and Rand

Gil and Bonnie Meredith

Joe and Laura Morris and children: Mabry and Tyson

Mary Selman (Mary Ellen Cook's mother)
Francine Stratton
Robin Sutton
Dorothy Wagner
Woody and Jenny White and children: Christen and Moriah
Ted and Shelby Whitson and daughter: Pam Whitson
Michael and Elizabeth Youssef and children: Sarah, Natasha, Joshua, and Jonathan

We started our singing with a lovely chorus, "Our God Reigns." It seemed just the right touch and the perfect music as we gave birth to The Church of The Apostles.

My eyes moistened several times during the service as I realized that God had given me the vision, and enough guidance and correction, to now stand in front of this small group of attendees. We had actually started The Church of The Apostles. It was finally a reality. "God, it's happened. You have done it. All I needed to do was trust and obey."

"We have come a long way," I said in one part of my sermon. "God has been with us. As joyful as life is and will be, I want you to remember that the road ahead is hard and will be filled with trouble. We may even have persecution from church leadership. But we know we are following God's will. We know we are moving on God's own timetable. This will give us comfort."

I had no idea how prophetically I had spoken.

***

The Church of The Apostles had a contract to use The Lovett facilities on Sundays, but we could not begin until September. I wished I had been sensitive enough to God to have asked them to allow us to start in May, and I expressed that to my wife.

"Don't be concerned," Elizabeth said, as she clasped my hand. "We have room to grow. By the time we move there in September, we'll need a building that large." She also reminded me that it was better to start with a small but solid group.

The following Friday, May 15, I received a call from John Sanders at St. Philip's. "You have a lot of friends at the Cathedral," he said. "Many of them have expressed a desire to have a commissioning service for you and the new church. We would like to do that."

I was genuinely touched. It seemed to me that it also would show the members of St. Philip's that we were starting a new church on good terms—that we were not trying to pull any of them with us, and that we intended to remain in fellowship with the Cathedral. We agreed to a commissioning service on Sunday, May 24.

***

May 17 was our second Sunday. By the time I arrived at our room at the Waverly, the place was packed. We couldn't fit them into that small space. At least sixty people had shown up. Fifty of them had a place to sit, and the remaining ten or more had to stand. Yet no one complained. In fact, they seemed pleased to have the problem. And it was a problem—a wonderful one—but still a problem. I conducted the service—and apologized to those who had to stand. Right then I knew we would need to make an immediate change. We needed a bigger space. We could rent a larger room, of course, or search for an entirely new location, but I didn't want to do either. Why not ask for permission to begin services at The Lovett School? The more I thought about it, the more obvious it seemed.

During the worship service, I announced, and asked them to spread the word that the following Sunday we would begin at

10:00, an hour later. That way, we could attend the commissioning service and be back in time for the worship service at the Waverly. Spontaneous applause broke out.

\*\*\*

John Sanders wrote a fine article in the Cathedral's weekly newsletter. In it, he said that the church must always be proclaiming the good news. He referred to me and my teaching at the Cathedral and my work with the Haggai Institute. Then he added:

> Now he has been led to establish and serve a mission congregation to the un-churched in the Vinings area. Michael has been kind enough to seek my advice and counsel about this project, and has put his vision under the authority of our Bishops and our diocesan Department of Mission Congregations. I now want us to support Michael and his new flock as this Cathedral has done for so many new congregations in the past. Our own Cathedral Evangelism Committee will stay in close touch with Michael and will let all of us know how and when we can help; one thing for sure—daily prayer for the success of this mission effort. As a congregation, we will officially send Michael and his family on their way with <u>special prayers this Sunday, May 24, at the 9:00 A.M. Eucharist.</u>

\*\*\*

On Sunday, May 24, we had the commissioning service. It was extremely well attended. I felt the warmth and support of the congregation, and I was grateful to Dean Sanders for suggesting the service.

Before the final prayer, I had a chance to address the worshippers. I spoke several minutes, mostly thanking them for their prayers and encouragement. I closed by saying, "Please do not leave the Cathedral and come to Apostles. I do not wish to harm one part of the kingdom just to build up another."

As I started to sit down, the people gave me a long, standing ovation—an expression of appreciation for five years of giving of myself and my time to minister there as a volunteer.

\*\*\*

A few days later I met again with Al Cash at The Lovett School. I had signed the contract for the chapel with just my own name, without any committee backing and without obligating any other people.

"Al, we've got a problem. We have already outgrown our own space at the Waverly."

"I know a lot of churches that would love that problem," he said and laughed.

"We need to move. Soon. Is it possible to start holding services at Lovett the first of June instead of September?"

"Shouldn't make any difference," he said, "but I'll have to go to the board."

"Of course," I said. "It just seemed foolish to move to a second place and then to move again before coming to Lovett."

Two days later we had approval to start services at Lovett on the first Sunday in June.

I would be in Germany the following week, so I asked Al to preach since he was an ordained Presbyterian minister. The Lovett chaplain was an Episcopal priest, so he agreed to celebrate communion.[7]

---

[7] In the Episcopal Church, only an Episcopal minister can celebrate the Eucharist.

\*\*\*

So many problems had been settled. But others soon arose. What about my work with the Haggai Institute? I loved what I was doing. I valued my relationship with John Haggai. John had been a friend and a mentor as well as my boss. Should I eventually plan to quit? Should I consider making myself only a part-time pastor? If I decided to leave, how could I tell John? A number of times he had spoken to me about succeeding him as the president of Haggai Institute when he retired. Would I be letting John down? He had been supportive of my endeavors to start a new church, but we had not spoken about my leaving the Institute.

While I was still trying to make a decision, I had to fly to Germany. John and I were planning to meet near Munich at the home of one of our board members.

After I arrived in Munich, John and I took a walk so we could talk. We discussed Institute matters, but then he asked, "How's the church going?"

"It is going so well, so much better than a lot of people expected. We're already packing the room full at the Waverly."

He asked a number of questions, showing his interest and concern in what I was doing. He must have thought about the possibility of my leaving, but we didn't bring it up.

During Apostles' first two services, someone had set up an inexpensive tape recorder to record our worship. I had brought a copy of the recordings with me, and I gave it to John. "Here are the first two sermons I preached at Apostles. We taped the whole service. It will give you an idea of how we are doing things."

"Thank you," John said. "I'll listen to it tonight when I go to bed."

We talked some more, and then we went back to the house where we were staying. Although I had been asking God for guidance about my relationship with the Haggai Institute, no answer had come. But now, after talking with John, I knew. No word, no special revelation, but a simple, peaceful assurance came to me. God wanted me to give myself full time to Apostles. If it was going to be the kind of global, impacting church that I had envisioned, I had to be able to give all my energy and time to make it happen.

I had to tell John, but I just didn't know how. The more I thought of breaking the news to him, the harder it became. That night, I had trouble getting to sleep. Finally, I prayed, "God, I belong to you and so does John. Both of us want your will. You're just going to have to work this out. And I know you'll do it in a way that will be good for both of us." Then, I turned over and slept peacefully all night.

The next morning after breakfast, John asked, "Can we go for a walk?"

"Sure." I assumed he had heard the tape, but I had no idea of his reaction.

"I listened to the tape," he said. "As a matter of fact, I listened to it several times." We walked in silence.

"I was touched," he finally said. "It wasn't so much the sermon, although that was excellent. I listened to you pray, and I listened to the prayers of others. It touched me to hear the many people who prayed for you and your family. I don't know if you remember, Michael, but one woman referred to you as 'our pastor.'"

I had not remembered her praying those words. John fell silent again. As we continued to walk, I nervously waited to hear the rest of his reaction.

"I prayed about this matter until one o'clock in the morning," he said in a quiet, low voice. "Finally, God gave me peace, and I went to sleep."

Again there was silence between us.

"I'll tell you what I'm going to do." He stopped, turned and faced me. "Michael, I'm going to release you. God has called you to be the pastor at Apostles. I hate to lose you, but I know this is right for you."

"Thank you, John," I said. His attitude and words touched me so deeply that tears flooded my eyes, and I didn't trust my voice. "Thank you," I was finally able to say again. Silently I thanked God for the gracious way this had worked out.

It was all coming together. Piece by piece. Problems vanished or got solved.

*God, I am so grateful that you have called me for this work. I promise that I'll be as faithful as I can to you—first and foremost—and to the people. And I know you will prosper the ministry of Apostles.*

*Help me to keep on trusting and obeying.*

*Chapter Seventeen*

## Serving God First

God had given Apostles an evangelistic vision. He had planted
our church so we could share the salvation of Jesus Christ with
others. But he did not leave us alone to accomplish that mission; in
fact, he took the lead in drawing others to Him.

From the early days of Apostles, many people became tearful
when they attended for the first time. Nominal Episcopalians—
cultural Christians who didn't really know the Lord—attended
because they were curious about this new Episcopal church. But
during the service, something moved within them. That something
brought tears to their eyes. When I spoke with them later, they
confessed that they did not know why they had cried. But I knew
why. It was the Holy Spirit.

At the end of each service, I would offer an invitation. "If
you've never committed your life to Jesus Christ, if you've never
been born of God, you can do that today."

I would take a few minutes to explain the gospel, and then we
would pray. While we prayed, I invited people who wanted to
commit their lives to Jesus to raise their hand. Only I could see
them. I didn't ask them to walk down front as with an altar call.
The chapel at Lovett was small, and I was sensitive to how
difficult it was for some people to make a public display. I did not

need to drag people out of their comfort zone. After all, it is the Holy Spirit that opens the eyes of the blind and draws us in. I did not need to do that.

Many people raised their hands during those prayers, often with tears running down their faces. I would always try to follow up with them later. Sometimes I followed up with them at their home, or other times, I invited them to meet me in the chaplain's office after the service.

One time, one of our members brought her elderly father with her to Apostles. John McCarty was 83 years old, a retired businessman whose wife was suffering from Alzheimer's. After my sermon, I invited people to accept Jesus as their Savior and John raised his hand.

Later, I called him and asked if I could pay him a visit. When we met, I said, "I noticed that you raised your hand during the service. Would you mind telling me about your decision?"

"I never understood what it meant to give your life to Christ until you explained it. I didn't understand that it was an individual choice."

John had been a Methodist and then an Episcopalian. But he didn't understand what they talked about at church. "It never made sense to me," he said.

I ministered to John and his wife and made many visits to their home. John's walk with the Lord gave him a powerful peace as he cared for his ailing wife. But he often regretted not accepting Jesus earlier in his life. "Why did it have to take me so long to understand?"

"We don't always know why," I would say, "but God's timing is always perfect."

John lived three more years. He had been a partner in Shaw Industries, and before he died, he donated $1 million in company stock to Apostles. "You're going to outgrow the chapel someday. You'll need to buy land and start building."

Another time, after I invited people to raise their hand and accept Jesus as their Savior, fourteen people showed up at my office. Two of the people were Cleve Meredith and his 17-year-old daughter, Emily. They both had raised their hands without knowing that the other had done so.

I spoke with them, and the other 12 people, and gave them some material to help them in their walk with the Lord. Cleve and Emily both began to read scripture and live in Christ.

At the time, Emily was very healthy—a bright young lady and a vivacious cheerleader. But a year later, she developed a brain tumor. She went in and out of hospitals for several years and then died at the too-young age of 21. But the Lord had known the number of Emily's days. He had drawn her to Him. And although Cleave suffered through the horrible tragedy of losing his daughter, the knowledge that Emily was with the Lord gave him great comfort.

There were many other stories of the Holy Spirit moving among those who started attending The Church of The Apostles.

There was Roy Jones, who had been a heavy drinker and reluctantly attended Apostles one Sunday on the insistence of his wife. He cried during the entire service. Later, he had no recollection of what the sermon or the songs were about. He only recalled that an overwhelming spirit had stirred within him. Roy later became a leader in our church and served as Rector's Warden one year.

There was Sam Ayoub, the CFO of Coca-Cola and a church man, but not born again. Sam gave his life to Christ at Apostles and also became a leader in the church. He would become a dear friend and father-figure to me.

There was Nick Chilivis, a brilliant attorney and former Revenue Commissioner for Georgia, who had thought that all religions were the same. At Apostles, he came into a relationship with Jesus Christ that transformed his life. He was a wise man with a powerful strength who would also become a great support for me.

From the first days of Apostles until today, the Lord has humbled me by the large number of people who have come to Christ, many of whom eventually served in the leadership of our church.

\* \* \*

When I was the executive vice president of the Haggai Institute, the administrative responsibilities had weighed me down. I worked on all of the institute's boards and traveled overseas frequently. I did the administration of the ministry instead of the ministry itself.

During that time, I felt the Lord saying, "This isn't what I called you to do. It's a great experience. I've trained you in the wilderness just like I did with Moses. But I've called you to proclamation, not administration."

Now that we had started The Church of The Apostles, the opportunity to work in the area of my calling gave me great joy. Yes, being a pastor was new to me. I had to make adjustments as I learned on the job. But knowing that I was following God helped me overcome any obstacles.

One adjustment I had to make was in dealing with second-guessing. When you run a parachurch organization like the Haggai Institute, you can make a decision and everyone will follow it. But in a church, a pastor's choices are often second-guessed: Why did you decide to do this? Why did you preach about that?

I didn't always handle the second-guessing in the godliest way. I'm sure I offended some people. Someone would question one of my decisions and suggest a different route, and I would say, "I'm not here to follow your opinion. I'm here to listen to God and follow Him."

Sometimes people would persist in pushing me in another direction. I would tell them, "This church is not for everyone. You need to visit other churches." I did not mean to offend anyone; I just didn't want them to spend their time being frustrated. And honestly, I didn't want to spend my time being aggravated.

Because I was following God's ideas, I felt confident that I did not have to compromise. I had seen pastors who always seemed to take the middle road to avoid offending anyone. But in the end, they offended everyone. I had decided that I wasn't going to do that. If everyone walked out of Apostles, that would be God's problem, not mine.

During those early days, some people left the church because I offended them. Now that I'm older, I've calmed down. If I had to do it all over again, I would be less uptight. But God was in charge, and He grew the church despite our imperfect ways. And as we grew, people accepted our mission and questioned my decisions less.

And boy did we grow! We had moved to the Lovett chapel because, at 60 people, we had maxed out our space at the Waverly. By mid-July—when so many people went away for the weekend or summer vacation—we were up to 75 people. By September, we were at 120.

From that point, with kids back in school and families back in their routines, our growth came even faster. On Christmas Eve, I looked up from the pulpit and was filled with awe. Six hundred people sat in the pews. Every seat was taken. The following year, we continued to average 400 attendees, so we started a second service. Soon we would average up to 700 people every Sunday.

Clearly, The Church of The Apostles filled a void. We were the only evangelical mainline church in Buckhead. We offered the uncompromising truth of Jesus Christ along with the familiar structure of the Episcopal Church. It was a rare combination, and that intrigued people.

\* \* \*

Although I had to deal with the occasional second-guessing, in general, the leadership and the congregation were very supportive of me.

When we started the church, Elizabeth and I had moved our family from Dunwoody to Buckhead. The public schools in the area were not very good, so we moved our children into private schools. Even with partial scholarships, the remaining tuition put a $25,000 dent in my family's annual budget.

I had to dig into my savings to pay our bills. Our savings dwindled. But I refused to ask for help. I was an independent person, and I felt I would rather die than ask for anything.

Once during a breakfast meeting, one of our leaders, Roy Ludwig, told me that my habitual reluctance to ask for help was really stubborn pride, not independence. I knew he had a point, but still I wouldn't tell anyone about my financial situation. I believed God would take care of my family and me.

Our savings were running out, however, and Elizabeth was worried. But then, right on schedule, the leadership figured out what was going on. Gene Hall called me one day and asked, "How are you living on what you're making?"

"God had blessed us with some savings," I said.

But my answer wasn't good enough for Gene. He hastily called a meeting of the leadership, and they agreed to adjust my salary.

From that time on, they stayed alert to what was going on with my financial situation.

\* \* \*

Apostles grew so quickly, and so many people came to the Lord, that I had to work very hard to keep up with the demands. To make matters worse, I had not learned to completely rely on God. Too often I considered myself to be a "manufacturer" instead of a "distributor." As a manufacturer, I felt the need to produce the fruits of God instead of recognizing that only God could produce His fruits.

By our third year, I was exhausted. Each day, I was on the run—I had a breakfast appointment, lunch appointment, dinner appointment, and five other appointments in between. Our children were young, and I was also trying to do my part as a father and husband. I ran myself into the ground—almost literally. I came down with double pneumonia.

But I thought I could handle even that. As a boy, I had faced several major illnesses, including typhoid and hepatitis. I figured double pneumonia would not be as big a deal as those. But after two days, I couldn't even get out of bed.

A friend of mine, Dr. Joe Woods, came to check up on me. I asked him to prescribe something to help with the symptoms—something that at least would enable me to walk the few steps to the bathroom.

Instead, Joe said, "You need to go to the hospital."

I did not want to go to the hospital; I had too much to do. But on the third day, I was no better. I realized there was nowhere else for me to look but up. I cried to the Lord, "I have so much that needs to be done! Please help me get better so I can get back to work."

But God seemed to say, "Now I've got your attention." Instead of helping me with my request, he told me, "You're running around trying to serve me, but you're not spending adequate time with me."

Of course God's word is always true, and He was speaking the truth to me. I had not been spending time with Him as I knew I should. Sometimes I was so rushed that I would not pray until I was in the car and fighting my way through morning traffic.

I cried, feeling the conviction of the Lord's words. "God, Teach me what You want me to do."

"I can do everything without you," He said. "But you cannot do a single thing without Me. You cannot minister to people before ministering to Me."

As I lay there, sick and unable to move, I spent more time talking with God. I asked, "How can I minister to You?"

Eventually I discerned the answer: through worship and praise.

I spent two weeks in bed, talking with God and slowly getting better. Once I recovered, I stopped scheduling breakfast appointments. Instead, I got up early every day and gave my first fruits to the Lord. I spent time in worship and praise, regardless of how long my to-do list was.

The result flabbergasted me. The tasks that would have taken days to finish now took hours. I was less haggard. I had more energy. By ministering to the Lord, He indeed helped me minister to others. I thanked God for that double pneumonia. It was through His mercy that He allowed me to get sick so I could learn one of the most important lessons of my life.

I believe that God blessed Apostles because I learned to see myself as His servant first. I turned to Him to fill me. What I can give people is nothing, but what He can give me is everything.

The leadership of the church learned that as well. During those early days, we would be severely tested as we defended the truth of God's word. Although we would make mistakes from time to time, we knew that God's faithfulness was perfect. We needed to rely on Him. We needed to serve Him first. If we worshipped and praised Him, if we trusted and obeyed Him regardless of the circumstances, then His work would be done through us.

*Chapter Eighteen*

**The New Conflict**

Since Apostles was an evangelical and an evangelistic
congregation, we were biblically conservative and opposed to the
liberal trends in the Episcopal Church. Whenever possible, we
raised our voices, even though few seemed willing to hear us. I
believed it was important to remain within the Anglican
Communion—to be a witness not only to the world around us, but
to those who were wavering or straying from a biblical faith.

Not once during those first three years did I talk about
becoming independent. I did not believe that course of action was
an option for us.

However, we were constantly conflicted about how to relate
and react to our denomination. The leaders of Apostles were
already asking questions: How much money do we keep
committing when we don't like the way it's being used? Why do
we continue to pour our money into projects that either ignore the
gospel or, as we felt, deny it? What should we do—what could we
do—to pull the Episcopal Church back to the fundamentals of the
faith?

I had no idea where the struggle was going to end. We needed
to find a resolution so we could use our energies to focus on God's
vision for evangelism and teach people how to live as Christians.

The denomination's strong pro-abortion stance and its support for the ordination of women had already upset our congregation.

And a far more explosive issue was to come.

\*\*\*

Before I had resigned from the Haggai Institute, one of the last things I agreed to do for them was to conduct a leadership training seminar in Hawaii. Even then, I had begun to express my concern about the direction the Episcopal Church seemed to be taking. Before I left for Hawaii, and while I was still there, I felt heavily burdened about Apostles and the Episcopal Church.

I prayed for guidance. Apostles was an infant congregation, and it was difficult enough to face our day-to-day issues without getting enmeshed in the problems that faced the entire Episcopal Church. As I prayed, I realized that we could not ignore our biblical differences. It became more and more obvious that our paths were moving in distinctly different directions. What could we do to put an end to those differences? How could we maintain our integrity and still be part of the Episcopal Church? While I was still in Hawaii and deeply involved in prayer, I heard about a church in Pittsburgh that had formed an independent board to own the church building and lease it to the church. That way, the Episcopal Church would not own the property.

*If it had worked for them, why couldn't it work for Apostles? Why couldn't our building be leased and not owned?* Such an arrangement would free us from the possibility of the Diocese pressuring us to conform to increasingly anti-biblical standards. But the idea scared me. Would that action muffle our voice in speaking to the wayward trends? Was it a wise thing to do? Was it some ambitious plan from my own heart or a message from God? I didn't know.

"God, is this the solution for us?" I prayed again and again. The more I prayed, the more sensible the idea sounded. Why not form a foundation that would own all properties of Apostles? Not wanting to rush into a decision, I considered every factor I could, both pro and con. No matter how many arguments I marshaled against it, I kept coming back to the idea.

Once I accepted it, then a concept really began to form in my mind. Why not set up a foundation? The board members would be conservative Christians, some of whom would not be Episcopalians. They would be trusted, faithful, and conservative believers. Then the foundation could lease its property to Apostles.

We needed some way to maintain our integrity and not be pressured into silence. But not only that, I wanted to open the door for funding from outside Episcopal sources. I sensed there were financially-able leaders who would not normally give to a building fund if the property was owned by a denomination. But they would give generously if they understood it as a biblical witness and that we would remain loyal to the gospel.

Setting up a foundation would work, but was it the right thing to do? Again and again I asked myself that question. The more I prayed about it and considered the implication, the more it did sound like the right thing. But I admitted that it was too big an issue to decide by myself. I wanted to share the concept with the lay leaders at Apostles. Because I believed in sharing the process with God's people, I was willing to trust them to pray, ponder, question, and discuss the vision.

First I spoke with Bill Bugg, Gil Meredith, and Gene Hall. All three men liked the idea very much. Then I broadened the circle so I could be sure we were considering this drastic step from every possible perspective.

I discussed the concept of a foundation with Wendell Byrd, a lawyer. His response was, "Michael, I think it's the best solution I've ever heard. Now you can go about God's work and not worry about the denomination taking the church away from you."

Wendell mentioned that other churches had done the same thing and had no problems when they pulled out of their denomination. He cited several Presbyterian congregations who had made the same kind of move before they pulled out of the Presbyterian Church (USA).

I wasn't considering the possibility of pulling out. I didn't want to do that. I wanted to form the foundation so we could *remain* part of the Episcopal Church.

Later, others would accuse me of plotting to leave. But I know the truth. More importantly, so does God.

*** 

We never seemed to have peace with the Diocese. Constant issues came up. We opposed each other on so many things. "Why does it have to be this way?" I kept asking God. "How can we concentrate on outreach and our own spiritual growth if we have to bicker with our leaders?" I complained to God that the very ones who were supposed to lead us to righteousness were leading us to unrighteousness.

Whenever I prayed and asked for a sign or some direct guidance, no answer came. Walls of silence closed around me. Maybe I was afraid of more controversy. I wanted a plan to develop in a way that I would not be perceived as schismatic.

Despite the continuing tension with the Diocese, The Church of The Apostles continued to grow. New members came into our congregation. Our membership by the end of 1988 was 400, with approximately 500 attending each week. Lives were being changed, and we felt we were making an impact among the leaders of Atlanta. But growing controversies with the Diocese wouldn't let up.

Finally, in January of 1989, I decided to talk to the Vestry. I had held back, not wanting to embroil them in any more of the controversial issues than necessary. But, after all, they had the fiduciary responsibility in the church. They deserved to know.

I went through the scenario of our theological differences with the Diocese. I laid it all out. When they understood the issues, I said, "You, as the Vestry, have to make a choice. Whatever you do is all right with me. I'll back you all the way. But at the same time, please hear this from me. I am convinced that it is God's will for us to establish a foundation. I'm not saying to you, 'Thus says the Lord,' only that this is a strong, inner conviction within me. If you go against what I'm suggesting, I'll love you as much as ever. I don't want you to do what I say just because I say it. Tonight I have come as a messenger who is here only to deliver a message. Do what you want with it. I want you to think about this, pray about it, and then meet together without me. I'm calling a special Vestry meeting next Sunday afternoon at 3:00 P.M. in Gene Hall's office."

I paused to make certain they got the time and date. Then I said, "I'm not going to be there. You debate it among yourselves, pray about it, and fight it out if you have to. But come back with a decision."

Whatever happens, I thought, it will be the right thing. I trusted those leaders to discern the mind of God.

*Chapter Nineteen*

**Separate Ways?**

The Vestry had their meeting in Gene Hall's office without me.
For more than three hours, they prayed about every aspect and
implication until everybody present felt they were in full harmony.
They concluded that it was not only right to establish a foundation,
but that it was the sensible thing to do. *Not one person dissented
on that issue.* When they left Gene's office at six, each of the
fifteen members was in total accord on everything.

That is, except for one man.

He didn't differ on the need for the foundation. He differed
purely on the approach and plan of action.

As it was later related to me, Joe Spence, a prominent
businessman, had said, "We're going to start a foundation. We've
agreed to that. Then let's do it now and get it over. I say we need
to go to the Bishop right away. We'll talk to him and say, 'This is
the way we're going to go. How will the Diocese respond?'"

"That's crazy," one of them answered.

"Why seek a confrontation when we don't have to?" another
voice responded.

"I want to go on record," Joe said. "I suggest that members of
the Vestry go to the Bishop right away and tell him our decision.

We'll tell him exactly why we're doing this. If he wants to kick us out, let him."

"No," the others insisted, "the better part of wisdom is to wait."

"Wait? And go through more sessions like this?"

After they talked more and prayed together, Joe knew that they had not changed their minds. To his credit, he agreed to go along with whatever decision the Vestry made.

They appointed three members of the Vestry—Bill Bugg, John Tyler, and Dave Lawton—to study the issue thoroughly and decide exactly how we would function as a foundation, how to implement the change of direction, and then how to make a presentation to the congregation and to the Bishop. They would also study other congregations who had done the very thing we were contemplating.

They contacted the church in Pittsburgh—Orchard Hill Church—that had given me the original idea, and they talked to the rector and several Vestry members. At that time, Orchard Hill Church was the fastest growing Episcopal Church in the country. I had thought they were unique in setting up a foundation within the Episcopal Church, although I heard that the practice was fairly common in England. As we learned later, other Episcopal congregations had already done the same thing.

At the committee's request, Orchard Hill Church sent us their foundation bylaws and the steps they had followed.[8] After careful study, the committee recommended that we adapt their bylaws to fit Apostles. The Vestry unanimously approved the recommendation.

---

[8] After we seceded from the Episcopal Church, they asked us to give them information on the process of leaving honorably and legally, and we willingly shared that material.

Before we set up a foundation, however, we needed to educate the congregation. Not wanting to cause unnecessary confusion and disruption, neither the Vestry nor I had made public statements about our problems with the Diocese. But most people knew from my preaching that we opposed the liberal direction in which the denomination was heading. Now was the time for the people who worshiped with us to become aware of our decisions and the reasoning behind them. So we called a special meeting with the congregation on July 17, 1989.

Then, acting on the advice of those I consulted, I made an appointment to see Bishop Allan. I told him that we wanted to form a foundation and that we would call it the Foundation of the Holy Apostles. He seemed surprised.

"We're a small congregation," I explained. "We have begun our ministry in an affluent, expensive area of town. We need support from outside the parish. As part of our concept, we want to involve other people—nonmembers of Apostles—to be on the board of the foundation. Of course, we will invite only those who share our evangelical conviction."

When I finished explaining what we had in mind, the Bishop asked several questions for clarification. Finally, he said, "Sounds like a good idea." He didn't give us permission, but he didn't oppose the idea.

Although I didn't say it, I made it clear by inference that we would be talking to prominent Christians in the business world and asking them to serve on the foundation. They would be people not affiliated with the Episcopal Church.[9] I hoped that would alleviate any fears that we would drain funds from other Episcopal churches.

---

[9] After leaving the denomination, having non-church members became unnecessary.

Immediately our lawyer began working on the nonprofit status. Meanwhile, to establish the foundation's board, I put together a list of individuals whom I felt were qualified to serve.

On January 17, 1990, Joe McCall, the then senior warden at Apostles, wrote and read aloud the following statement for the members of our congregation, reviewing some of our past history. Here is part of that statement:

> Since its inception in 1987, The Church of The Apostles, in Atlanta, Georgia, has been recognized as being global in its vision, evangelical in its theology, and Anglican/Episcopalian in its affiliation.

> When its Founding Rector sought permission from the Diocese of Atlanta to form the congregation, he wrote that it would be Evangelical in its proclamation of the Gospel.

> Certainly the phenomenal growth of The Church of The Apostles, with its global view of missions, has been a clear indication of God's blessings and approval of our following the vision which He created.

> Given the global nature of Apostles, coupled with prohibitive prices of land and building in our assigned area, we believe that God has given us a solution. That is, friends of the church brought about the formation of a separate nonprofit foundation, the Foundation of the Holy Apostles, Inc. This organization is broad in scope and is inclusive of both members

and non-members of the church, and yet is committed to the Anglican tradition.

This charitable foundation will take the burden of raising funds far and wide, within and without The Church of The Apostles and the Episcopal Church as a whole. The concept is this . . . building a church facility and then leasing it for a long term, at less than cost, to the congregation of The Church of The Apostles. This naturally follows the unanimous decision of the Vestry of The Church of The Apostles in March 1989, to be a leasing congregation. In this matter the church can devote its budget and energies to its mission, leaving the need for a building in the hands of the Trustees of the Foundation of the Holy Apostles.

. . . This mission is not only about seeking a suitable site or facility for a permanent home for The Church of The Apostles, but is also about raising the necessary funds from individuals and foundations.

This is an arduous task, yet with the power, blessing, and leadership of the Holy Spirit, we are on the road to achieving our goals . . . .

\*\*\*

We had not tried to operate in secret and had consciously done everything as publicly as we knew how. But one day the Bishop seemed to wake up and realize the implications of our action. I assumed that somebody had asked, "Don't you understand what this means? By setting themselves up as a foundation, they are actually making themselves independent. In doing that, they are putting themselves outside the control of the Diocese. They can pull the church out of the Diocese any time they choose."

So far as I understood, that realization of our plan occurred when the Foundation of the Holy Apostles submitted a proposal to buy property on Mt. Paran Road in northwest Atlanta.

When the Bishop heard that the foundation wanted to buy property, he was upset. He phoned me and let me know quite firmly of his opposition. "Michael, I will not consecrate this." He insisted that he would not agree to be any part of what we were doing.

He wrote several letters, including one that said, "I cannot and will not give my consent to the establishment of an Episcopal congregation in any location where the title to the permanent building is not held by the parish in trust for the Episcopal Diocese of Atlanta."

In a written reply from the Vestry, we made our position clear: "If the foundation acquires the site at Interstate 75 and Mt. Paran Road, and offers Apostles a lease of the new building proposed to be erected thereon, we will, indeed, be fortunate, and our present intention is to accept such a lease."

Eventually, the foundation's bid for the property fell through. But the occasion stirred up the forces against us. As one member of the Vestry said, "The gauntlet has been thrown."

*Chapter Twenty*

## Toward the End?

The Triennial General Convention is a big event in the Episcopal Church. As the name implies, it happens only every third year. Delegates from across the church meet for ten days and make decisions of policy and canon (binding church laws) that affect the entire church. The convention that met in Phoenix in July 1991 was the one that brought our problems into the open.

Most of us on the Vestry assumed how the delegates would vote. We wanted to be wrong. Unfortunately, our assumptions proved to be correct.

One hopeful note occurred when Bishop William Frey from Ambridge, Pennsylvania, tried to get through a canon that would require all clergy to abstain from sexual relations outside of marriage. But it was defeated. More than eight hundred deputies, both clergy and laity, along with two hundred members of the House of Bishops, defeated the proposal. To us at Apostles, and to many conservatives, it clearly showed that the Episcopal Church no longer saw sexual activities as intended only between husband and wife. Primarily, the canon was defeated because it would have ruled against all homosexual activity.

After defeating Frey's motion, the convention adopted a compromise that was, as one report said, "Generally gay friendly."

They also passed a resolution that both clergy and laity should begin to educate members about lesbian and gay issues and to make a report at the next general convention.

Other actions taken at the convention included:

- The ordination of homosexuals came to the floor. The convention compromised by agreeing to study the situation for three more years.
- A number of bishops stated they intended to ordain practicing homosexuals. Some had been doing so for years.
- The House of Deputies issued a report to Episcopal schools that stated: "It is important for schools to hire openly gay and lesbian teachers to serve as role models."

In his reflections on the convention, John H. Rodgers, the then Director of Stanway Institute for World Mission and Evangelism, wrote that the convention made "crystal clear that we would not approve a moratorium on ordaining persons of active homosexual lifestyle." Then he asked, "Why not include and ordain non-monogamous, hetero-sexually active persons, too? If we can't draw a line here in so plain a matter as this, one wonders if there are any lines we can draw."

For background, here are instances of the ordination of homosexuals, all done with full knowledge of the individual's sexual orientation.

1. In December 1989, Bishop of Newark, John Spong, ordained openly homosexual Robert Williams to the priesthood.
2. In 1990, Walter Righter, assistant to Bishop Spong, ordained a homosexual man to the deaconate.
3. In 1991, Ronald Haines, Bishop of Washington, D.C., ordained a lesbian to the priesthood.

4.   At the 1991 Triennial Convention, Bishop Spong said he had welcomed eight practicing homosexual priests into his Diocese.

5.   At the same convention, Bishop Spong stated that within the previous three years, nine dioceses had ordained practicing homosexuals: New York, Pennsylvania, Michigan, Washington, D.C., California, Los Angeles, Minnesota, Chicago, and Newark.

Once the reports came to us from the Triennial Convention, our congregation was in an uproar. "What are we going to do about this?" many asked. Members expressed feelings of betrayal from the leaders of our church.

Then the Episcopal Bishop of Atlanta wrote a letter to all clergy, dated July 14, 1991. I'm sure he intended his letter to be conciliatory and informative. To us at Apostles, it only fanned the flames of pain and anger. The letter contained one paragraph that particularly upset us:

> The Episcopal Church has historically been a moderate church, the via media [i.e., the middle way or middle of the road], not because the moderate way is the lowest common denominator, but because more often than not the truth lies in the middle way, in the syntheses of the two polarities which the middle way seeks to embrace. Those who are not comfortable with ambiguity will, in the meantime, wish for more definitive closure, but I believe that the way of the Gospel is to follow Jesus Christ through the wilderness to a deeper

understanding of what it means to "walk in
newness of life."

I can't express how troubled I became over that letter. In my
mind, the Bishop had denied the integrity of the Bible and of our
faith. Although I felt the betrayal personally, I also realized it was
not a battle between Michael Youssef and the Diocese of Atlanta.
The battle involved all of us at Apostles.

Before taking any action, I believed that everyone at Apostles
ought to know exactly what the Bishop had written. I didn't want
any statements made that we couldn't prove. So we made copies of
the pastoral letter and distributed it to every member of the Vestry.
That was the best way I knew to let them deal with facts without
rumors or innuendoes.

At the next Vestry meeting, the leaders were all concerned, and
some were quite angry about the path the church was pursuing.

"What does God want us to do?" they asked each other. The
Vestry debated a long time until one of them finally gave us a
sense of direction. Our direction was to go directly to the Bishop
and tell him, "We want to introduce a resolution at the next
Diocesan Council."

Subsequently, the Vestry prepared a resolution that read as
follows:

> Resolved that the Diocese affirm the Word
> of God revealed through the Holy Scriptures
> that sexual relations are to be conducted
> only through holy matrimony.

Then, in our letter to the Bishop, we explained that we sought
to have our resolution introduced at the next Diocesan Council.
We also stated that "unless and until" they passed such a
resolution, we would "drastically reduce giving to the mission of

the Diocese." In 1990, we had given them $100,000 and the following year we had contributed $60,000.

Before the North Atlanta Convocation convened, where we hoped to have our resolution read, Bishop Allan called me. He said our resolution would "never pass at the Diocesan Council." He went on to say, "I'll throw out the resolution. I'll use the power of my chair to throw it out."

Despite his response, all fifteen members of the Vestry signed a letter that we hoped would still bring the matter up for debate. But as we had expected, the convocation failed to endorse our resolution. That meant we could not bring it to the floor for debate.

A year earlier, in November 1990, I had stood at the Diocesan Council when they were debating the same issue. I explained what the Bible said on the subject so everyone could understand that the church was heading away from God's word.

A veteran layman, a man who had been a council delegate for many years listened and then stood up to ask, "Does the Bible really say all that?"

"It certainly does," I said.

"I've never read the Bible," he said, "so I didn't know."

His attitude was similar to many. I had left that meeting with a heavy heart. Now a year later, as the situation deteriorated, my heart was broken even more.

The battle with the Diocese never reached a cease-fire agreement. I tried at times to reach out to those who opposed our stance. But that did no good.

\*\*\*

## VESTRY LETTER – AUGUST 12, 1991

 **The Church Of The Apostles**

*Meeting Place • The Lovett School Chapel • 4075 Paces Ferry Road, NW • Atlanta, Georgia 30327*
*Mailing Address • 4200 Paces Ferry Road • Suite 365 • Atlanta, Georgia 30339 • 404-435-4350*

*The Reverend Michael Youssef, Ph.D. Founding Rector*

August 12, 1991

The Rt. Rev. Frank K. Allan
Bishop of Atlanta
The Episcopal Diocese of Atlanta
2744 Peachtree Road, N.W.
Atlanta Georgia  30363

Dear Bishop Allan:

We were shown a copy of your letter to the clergy of the Diocese in which you have outlined your assessment of the National Convention.

We are deeply saddened that the 1991 Convention has failed to take a clear cut Biblical stand on many of the issues, including the ordination of practicing homosexuals and the use of inclusive language when referring to the Trinity. However, we are most concerned by the entire theological approach which the hierarchy of the Episcopal Church has taken on matters of faith and morals.

In your letter you state that " more often than not the truth lies in the middle way" and indicate that the clergy and communicants should be comfortable with "ambiguity", awaiting the "insight as is necessary from theologians, theological ethicists, social scientists, and gay and lesbian persons ..." The "middle way" unfortunately means the middle way between the Word of God as expressed in the Holy Scripture, and temporal human experience expressed by the insights of the above mentioned groups.

We wish to record our utter disapproval of placing temporal human experience on the same level as (or, even, superseding) the eternal truth of the Holy Scripture.

As a result of the failure in leadership created by the Church hierarchy, this Vestry is exercising its responsibility under Biblical authority for the leadership of our congregation. The Vestry of The Church of The Apostles will, therefore, introduce a resolution at this year's Diocesan Council reaffirming that this Diocese stands on the Word of God, and not on the experience of man, on these issues. Furthermore, we will work diligently with other vestries in the Diocese to have this resolution passed. Unless and until that resolution is passed, we will drastically reduce our pledge to the mission of the Diocese.

It is our prayer and desire that the National Church and our Diocese return to the authoritative Word of God and the Anglican Doctrine which affirms that Word without "ambiguity".

Sincerely,

THE VESTRY
THE CHURCH OF THE APOSTLES

The Rt. Rev. Frank K. Allan
August 12, 1991

## BISHOP'S LETTER – AUGUST 30, 1991

### THE EPISCOPAL DIOCESE OF ATLANTA

2744 Peachtree Road, N.W. - Atlanta, Georgia 30363
Telephone (404) 365-1016 - FAX (404) 261-2515 - GA Toll Free (800) 537-6743

The Rt. Rev. Frank K. Allan
Bishop of Atlanta

August 30, 1991

The Vestry
Church of the Apostles'
4200 Paces Ferry Road, Suite 365
Atlanta, Georgia 30339

I am sorry to hear that you were saddened by the results of the 1991 General Convention. Certainly no one got what they wanted, but I believe that the Holy Spirit was present and guiding us in our deliberations. I do not know of anyone who would suggest that the "middle way" means "the middle way between the Word of God as expressed in Holy Scripture and temporal human experience." Anglicans have always held to the "middle way" not because it is the lowest common denominator but because it is the Truth of God as revealed by scripture, tradition, and reason.

It saddens me that you would withhold support for the mission of the Diocese of Atlanta - our ministry to the poor, campus ministry, aid to parishes, support of our conference center and the world-wide mission of our church - "unless and until 'a resolution is passed'" which expresses the truth of the Gospel in terms that are acceptable to you.

In order to continue in dialogue without us being swayed by whether or not the Church of the Apostles' will provide financial support to our Diocese, we will not include any anticipated support from the Church of the Apostles' in our 1992 budget plans.

Sincerely yours,

Frank K. Allan
Bishop of Atlanta

FKA/gs

Three years earlier, I had a lengthy telephone call and then a personal meeting with the Bishop that lasted two and a half hours. The gist of the meeting was that he insisted I accept the ordination of women and become part of the mainstream of the Episcopal Church.

Previously I had written an article on why I didn't support the ordination of women. In my book, *Leading The Way*, I included a chapter in which I explained my position about women in church leadership. My position—and I believed it was biblical—was that women can be involved in all areas of the life of the church except pastoral oversight—the role of pastor or rector.

When I refused to change, the Bishop said, "I can tell you this much. You will not be accepted and Apostles will not be accepted."

"I understand," I said, "and I'm sorry for the position you are taking. But my conviction is biblical orthodoxy."

When I write of that meeting, I can only give my impressions, of course. I perceived the Bishop as being extremely angry with me. For those two and a half hours, I felt as if he was a boxer and I had become his punching bag. The words I most remember, however, were when he said, "Michael, you are out of the mainstream. You need to get out of the Episcopal Church if you cannot willingly accept its direction!"

Had I realized it, I had already reached the end. I didn't see it that way, of course, and I didn't want to see it that way. I had not yet been able to accept the fact that I might one day have to sever my relationship with the Episcopal Church. It was still an unthinkable choice.

Yet somewhere deep inside, perhaps even then, I knew that an eventual rupture with the Diocese had to take place. When I started Apostles, my hope had been that we could proclaim the gospel, reach the cultural Christians (the South is full of them), strengthen believers, and share Christ with others. At the same time, I naïvely hoped that it could be like my experiences in Australia. We did the Lord's work and the denomination encouraged us. Bishops in Sydney were constantly exhorting us to righteous living founded on biblical principles.

I didn't expect people with opposing viewpoints to back us, but I did hope they would leave us alone.

I was naïve.

*Chapter Twenty-One*

**The Final Rupture**

After the Triennial Convention, I had wanted—but not really expected—to be able to discuss our differences with the Bishop. His letter did nothing, whether he intended to or not, to help us continue in dialogue. My assumption then—and still today—is that he was not going to make any effort to reconcile our differences. If we compromised, he would accept us. If we maintained our biblical stance, we would be alone and without his support. Maybe the Bishop was wise enough to realize that it would never be possible for Apostles and the Diocese of Atlanta to arrive at an accommodation.

After receiving the Bishop's letter, our Vestry faced an exceptionally heated discussion. Although present, I chose not to enter into the debate. "You have to make your decision on how to handle this without me," I said. "But if I feel I have to interject something, I'll tell you." At that point I handed the chair to the senior warden.

During the discussion, one strong voice said, "Within the Diocese there are a lot of lay people in church leadership who feel the way we do. Let's bypass the clergy and mobilize the laity. Ask them to join us to fight this clerical drift."

"It won't work," I spoke up. "Don't do it."

"We can make it work. We'll really put on the pressure—"

"I beg you not to do this."

"We're right in what we believe," another said. "We need to stand up for our faith."

"It won't work." I understood their anger and felt it as well. Although I applauded their wanting to take a stand, I knew they were going about it in a nonproductive way. "This is a clerical church, not a lay church," I pointed out. "By our very structure, the power resides in the Bishop, don't forget that. You won't mobilize the laity. You can't. In fact, they'll misunderstand what you're trying to do."

They listened, but I did not change their minds. They went ahead and drafted the letter that essentially called for the lay people to revolt. They sent copies to every senior and junior warden of the 88 Episcopal Churches in the Diocese of Atlanta. They also enclosed copies of the church's correspondence with the Bishop.

Although I personally opposed what they were doing, I didn't feel I should exert undue influence on that body to stop them. Yet I knew the repercussions would come.

I knew I would receive the brunt of them.

And I wasn't mistaken.

\*\*\*

## VESTRY LETTER TO DIOCESE OF ATLANTA – AUGUST 12, 1991

 # The Church Of The Apostles

*Meeting Place • The Lovett School Chapel • 4075 Paces Ferry Road, NW • Atlanta, Georgia 30327*
*Mailing Address • 4200 Paces Ferry Road • Suite 365 • Atlanta, Georgia 30339 • 404-435-4350*

*The Reverend Michael Youssef, Ph.D. Founding Rector*

August 12, 1991

Dear Fellow Members of the Diocese of Atlanta:

We recently received a copy of the enclosed letter written by Bishop Frank Allan to all of the clergy in our Diocese. As the lay leaders of our Church, we cannot believe that our National and Diocesan hierarchy has moved so far away from the inspired Word of God as the basis of our beliefs and our actions.

We cannot believe that the National hierarchy rejected an affirmation that sexual relations of clergy should be conducted only within holy matrimony.

We cannot believe that it is the stated intention of some bishops to ordain practicing homosexuals in direct contradiction of Biblical standards of morality. And that a resolution for even a moratorium on such actions was soundly defeated.

We cannot believe that the convention approved a resolution to continue the development of inclusive language liturgies which use feminine and neutered images of God, in direct contradiction of His revealed nature from Scripture.

Recognizing our own sinful nature and painfully aware of our own imperfections, we nevertheless were so disturbed by these movements away from the revealed Word of God that we have written a letter to the Bishop, which we have also enclosed.

We urge you to read both letters yourself and prayerfully to consider whether our Episcopal Church should stand on the Word of God or on the experience of man.

We would like to send members of our Vestry to meet with your Vestry within the next thirty days . Given the confessed failure of leadership of our National hierarchy, we believe that our lay leadership must fill this vacuum; and do so quickly.

Very truly yours,

THE VESTRY
THE CHURCH OF THE APOSTLES

Despite their miscalculation in trying to mobilize the laity, the Vestry wisely realized our congregation needed to know what was happening. We were unfortunately heading for the big gunfight at the O.K. Corral, and we wanted to make certain they knew what our stand was about.

A few days later, we mailed a letter to everyone involved in The Church of The Apostles.

***

## VESTRY LETTER TO "My Fellow Apostles" – AUGUST 16, 1991

 **The Church Of The Apostles**

*Meeting Place • The Lovett School Chapel • 4075 Paces Ferry Road, NW • Atlanta, Georgia 30327*
*Mailing Address • 4200 Paces Ferry Road • Suite 365 • Atlanta, Georgia 30339 • 404-435-4350*

*The Reverend Michael Youssef, Ph.D. Founding Rector*

August 16, 1991

*My Fellow Apostles*

As you are aware, the National Convention of the Episcopal church was recently held in Phoenix, Arizona. Our Bishop Allan has written to the clergy of the Diocese, outlining his views on the Convention and we attach a copy of his letter.

In the resolution attached to Bishop Allan's letter, the Convention admitted its "failure to lead" the church. As a result, your Vestry has concluded that it must exercise its responsibility under Biblical authority to provide leadership to our congregation.

Both before and during the convention, a number of Bishops stated their intention to ordain openly practicing homosexuals, in direct contradiction of the Word of God. And, a proposed three-year moratorium on such actions was soundly defeated in the House of Deputies; we understand that the bishops refused even to impose a short moratorium. It would seem, therefore, that the current leadership of the Episcopal Church intends to allow de facto ordination of homosexuals.

The House of Deputies defeated, by 141 votes to 87, a new canon which sought to affirm that all clergy should abstain from sexual relations outside of holy matrimony. As Bishop Allan has stated in his letter, the House of Bishops did not consider this resolution. However, the House of Bishops subsequently defeated, by 93 votes to 84, a proposed amendment (to Resolution A-104) that contained similar language and which called upon its "bishops, priests and deacons to abstain from sexual relations outside of marriage".

The Convention also approved the continued development of liturgies which use feminine and neutered images of God - in direct contradiction of His revealed nature from scripture (A-121). The house of Deputies also resolved to direct the widespread distribution to Episcopal schools of a report on youth which, among other assertions, states, "it is important for schools to hire openly gay and lesbian teachers to serve as role models ...." (D-050).

Your Vestry of The Church of the Apostles, condemns and rejects the above actions and the leadership which sponsored them! As for this Church, we will continue to rely on the Bible and the Holy Spirit as the source of all wisdom.

In our reply to Bishop Allan, a copy of which is enclosed, we have stated that we will seek to have a resolution passed at the next Diocesan Council to be held in November, reaffirming that this Diocese relies on the Word of God and not on the experience of man. Unless and until such a resolution is passed, we have informed the Bishop that we will drastically reduce our pledge to the mission of the Diocese.

The Vestry decided unanimously to write this letter to the Bishop, following two special meetings, and only after deep prayer. Every one of the Wardens, both past and present, have endorsed the Vestry's decision.

If you have any questions or concerns, I will be very happy to attempt to answer them for you. In the meantime, we seek your prayers on behalf of our Rector and our Church. Pray that we may continue to grow in the grace and knowledge of our Lord Jesus Christ. To Him be the glory both now and forever.

Sincerely,

A. Anthony McLellan
Senior Warden

I had expected trouble and repercussions.

I got even more than I expected.

I was overwhelmed by the vehement response. As I predicted, lay leaders misread the Vestry's action; most of them didn't understand the letter. The wardens handed their letter to their rectors and essentially asked, "What is all this? I don't know anything about this homosexual stuff."

For the next few weeks, I received the most abusive phone calls and letters I've ever gotten from clergy.

In the first section of a two-page letter from a rector, I read these words: "In essence, having flung off the protective cover of an accountable authority you have exposed yourself to demonic attack which you will not be able to withstand regardless of how biblical, Spirit-filled, and dedicated you are."

One anonymous letter read simply: "Galatians 3:3. Are you so foolish? After beginning in the Spirit, are you now trying to attain your goal by human effort?"

Although I wasn't positive what the writer meant to say, I assumed it was a rebuke to us for our action. It was one person's way of saying that we were resorting to human efforts. I thought it strange that the person would use a quotation from the Bible. After all, the authority of the Bible had been the basic issue in conflict.

From another rector came a particularly caustic letter. One passage read: "Your position gives new and abysmal meaning to the Word *evangelical*, focused mainly on making Christianity as forbidding and puritanical as possible. If that is your idea of the 'scandal of the Gospel,' I want no part of it."

As I read that letter and the many others, I felt sad and depressed, even though I had known such responses would come. And to some extent, I understood their position. Our Vestry had taken a courageous step, but it was one that went against Episcopal practice.

Many members of the Vestry came from congregational churches and did not understand the hierarchical nature of the Episcopal Church. As much as I tried not to take the angry words personally, they did affect me. For weeks, I spent many days and nights troubled over the issue.

At the same time, however, I received a lot of support from members of Apostles, as well as calls and letters of encouragement from other congregations. Some agreed with our position although they disagreed with our procedure.

All in all, it was a tense time. If nothing else, I think the Vestry's decision brought the major issues into the open. No matter what we did (or didn't do), the result eventually would have been the same. Of that I'm certain. Our actions simply sped up the process.

In reflection, maybe what the Vestry did was necessary to stir themselves and to make other lay people aware of how strongly we felt. We could have left the scene quietly, and few people outside Apostles would have known the truth. Maybe the letter to church wardens was our last act of witness among the organized Episcopal Church of our stance for the biblical faith.

***

During our next Vestry meeting, I said, "Look, I've become the target. I'm getting a lot of letters and phone calls. They're not calling or writing to you. They're writing to me. In the past two weeks, I've been called every name in the book." I held up a stack of letters and read portions from them. They heaped blame on me for all the turmoil.

Although some of them were simply hostile and angry, I almost wept as I read one rector's letter. Although I could not give the Vestry his name, I read how he agreed with our position, but felt he had to back down. His letter concluded, "My people are turning against me. I've only got a couple more years before retirement. I just want to finish up and retire in peace."

I don't remember what I said after reading the final sentence, but my heart was heavy. Then I paused. I could tell from their expressions that the members of the Vestry had not realized what serious repercussions their letter would bring.

"We didn't know," one of them said. "We just didn't believe that you would get such opposition."

"The other wardens didn't even want to understand what we were trying to say, did they?" asked another.

"Now you know," I said. Until then, I'm sure they thought I was exaggerating the seriousness of the problem.

"What do we do?" asked a member. "We're behind you, Michael, and we want to share the flak."

"Let's not take any action right now," I said. "Let's pray and fast for 36 hours. We'll meet Saturday morning to break our fast and hear what the Lord has to say. Until then, let's pray and get away from the world as much as possible. If each of us asks God for direction, the Lord will tell us what to do."

As I prayed during the next 36 hours, I thought about how the Vestry was composed of some of the godliest people I had ever known. Yet at the same time, I felt as if God was saying, "I still want to do something important through this congregation, but I cannot do it as long as you are a part of this Diocese. Apostasy can have no fellowship with truth." Just then, I thought of the words of Jesus when he said that new wine cannot be poured into an old wine skin. The reason for that, of course, was that the new wine ferments and expands. The old, worn skin can't take change and it bursts open.

"Lord, I'm not going to say this to them," I prayed. "You have to do it. If what I am feeling is your will, then you make it clear to them."

I did not know what was going to happen. But I knew God was going to guide us. The members of the Vestry prayed and fasted as I had requested. On Saturday morning, I felt even stronger that it was time for us to leave the Diocese, but I just couldn't say those words aloud.

After we came together, we had a wonderful time. We worshipped, we sang. Tears came to many eyes as we opened our hearts to God and to each other.

Finally, it was time to talk. "Do any of you feel the Lord is leading us one way or the other?" I asked. "If you do, speak up. If you have heard the Lord correctly, the others will confirm it."

"I prayed, and here is what I think," said Dr. Mike McDevitt, a prominent oral surgeon who served as a junior warden in 1993 and continues to be a wonderful member and a friend. "It's like this. As I prayed, I felt God saying that he had already told you what we should do."

"That's exactly what I sensed," said Joe McCall, who was senior warden in 1990.

Parker Hudson (junior warden in 1990) and Joe Morris (senior warden later in 1992) spoke up and said that they also had sensed that God had already told me what to do. Byron Attridge, junior warden that year, said, "You are our leader, so lead us in this."

Those were not the words I had wanted to hear. I was begging the Lord not to make me speak. I just didn't want to be accused of planning from the beginning to pull the church out and forcing it on anybody.

Finally, I said, "I think God wants us to shake the dust off our feet."

Parker Hudson, a third-generation Episcopalian and the person on the Vestry who had been the most opposed to our leaving, said, "I want to have the privilege of making the motion that we pull out of the Episcopal Church."

I was so touched to hear him speak those words. Parker would never have considered, let alone made a motion, for us to leave the church of his family if he had not been convinced God was leading us. Tears filled my eyes, and I couldn't say anything at first. Inwardly, I was saying, "God, thank you, thank you for doing it this way."

Joe McCall seconded the motion.

After that, we had virtually no discussion. Every one of the fourteen present (Polly Peacock, the fifteenth member, was absent due to family illness) voted to leave our denomination.

Before taking any action, our church lawyer who was there, told us that the bylaws said we had to announce a meeting and then wait 15 days. That is, announce it for two consecutive Sundays and then have the meeting.

We announced to the congregation that we were going to "discuss our future" in regards to the Diocese of Atlanta.

We said nothing about leaving.

*Chapter Twenty-Two*

## A Crucial Meeting

I didn't look forward to meeting with Bishop Allan.

I wasn't concerned; I was just tired of the fighting. By the beginning of October 1991, I knew there was no way for The Church of The Apostles to be at peace with the Diocese.

I took the two wardens to the meeting with me. It lasted two hours.

"I want to apologize unreservedly for the Vestry," I said. "For any presumed discourtesy they showed in writing directly to other vestries. They were not trying to do anything underhanded."

The senior warden also apologized for the strong words in the letter to the Bishop, specifically the line: "Unless and until a motion is passed, we will withhold funds."

Our apologies and openness did not seem to be enough, however. As we continued to talk, the Bishop again demanded that we dissolve the Foundation of the Holy Apostles. He was intractable about that. The three of us were just as adamant in standing our ground.

Finally, the junior warden, Byron Attridge, said that the matters of foundation, ordaining women, and homosexuality were not the real issues we were fighting about. "The real issue that divides us is that the hierarchy of the Episcopal Church does not accept the Bible as the inerrant Word of God. From this difference comes the problem."

The Bishop fully agreed, but contended that the Bible was open to many interpretations.

The senior warden then said, "I think our position is clear. We don't belong in the Episcopal Church anymore. You want us out, don't you?"

"I would never kick you out," the Bishop said.

"But you don't want us to stay."

"I will not accept you if you refuse to dissolve the foundation."

"Our congregation is meeting October 13," I said. "At that time, we will discuss our relationship to the Diocese." I don't recall saying we would vote to pull out, but the Bishop knew that was what I meant.

Then the tone of the meeting changed. Once it was obvious we were going to leave, and he concurred with that decision, the Bishop became extremely helpful. He went so far as to promise that he would help me maintain my Episcopal ordination and assist in a smooth transfer of the present retirement plan and health insurance for the staff.[10]

The Bishop discussed with us the mechanics of leaving the Diocese. "I assure you that I will do everything possible to make your transition as smooth as possible." Through the lengthy conversation, the Bishop understood and agreed that we would form a new corporation and transfer all the present assets of The Church of The Apostles into it.

\*\*\*

Reporters began calling us. "We would like to be in the meeting," they said. Even though I was surprised they wanted to

---

[10] As I realized later, however, those were only promises. Unfortunately he did not follow through on them.

attend—it had not occurred to me that our decision was important to the public media—I explained that it would be a meeting for members only. As I learned later, the Bishop had sent out a press release announcing that Apostles was pulling out of the Diocese. Although I don't know the Bishop's motive, my feeling was then, and still is today, that he wanted us out but didn't want to be blamed for pushing us out. He had the authority to excommunicate us, but that was not what bishops did.

Despite the possible attendance by members of the press and a few other on-lookers, we went ahead with our plans for the congregational meeting. Our lawyer would make a formal transcript of the meeting.

A major concern of mine was that I didn't want the Vestry or me to push the congregation into anything. We hoped that once we had clarified our position, they would understand the gravity of the situation. We were willing to trust God to speak to them.

We had scheduled the meeting for Sunday morning, October 13, 1991. The Bishop faxed me a letter on Friday and asked if I would read it before we voted.

Here is the content of the letter, which the senior warden read to the congregation before we started to debate:

'91-10-11 10:54 DIOCESE

## THE EPISCOPAL DIOCESE OF ATLANTA

2744 Peachtree Road, N.W. · Atlanta, Georgia 30363
Telephone (404) 365-1016 · FAX (404) 261-2515 · GA Toll Free (800) 537-6743

The Rt. Rev. Frank K. Allan
Bishop of Atlanta

October 11, 1991

To: The Rector, Wardens, Vestry, and Congregation of the Episcopal
    Church of the Apostles'

Grace to you and peace from God our Father and the Lord Jesus
Christ.

My prayers are with you this hour as you seek to decide whether
to remain in union with the Diocese of Atlanta, the Episcopal Church
and the worldwide Anglican Communion.

It is my hope that you will remain committed to the doctrine,
discipline and worship of the Episcopal Church, but should you decide
otherwise, you will continue to have my support and prayers for your
mission and ministry.

As there is but one Lord, one faith, one baptism, one God and
Father of us all, I know that we can pray together the Prayer for
Unity in the Book of Common Prayer that "we will be all of one heart
and of one soul, united in one holy bond of truth and peace, of faith
and charity, and may with one mind and one mouth glorify God through
Jesus Christ our Lord."

Faithfully yours,

+ Frank K. Allan
Bishop of Atlanta

FKA/gs

156

I'm not sure those outside a denomination like ours could have understood the severity of what we were considering. Even though it has become commonplace in the last few years, in those days congregations simply did not leave the Episcopal Church. Because the power was vested in the Bishop and not the laity, this was a bold and courageous step for lay people to take.

When our members came to the meeting, most of them were surprised. Few had any idea what we meant by "discuss our future." Of course, they had been aware of tension with the Diocese. But some of them were so firmly rooted in Episcopalian soil that they would not agree to leave, regardless of the reasons. They liked the worship and the people at Apostles, but that was not as important to them as their religious heritage.

The senior warden gave a report on the history of our difficulties with the Diocese. He then explained that the entire Vestry, after a time of prayer and fasting, had unanimously agreed to terminate our relationship with the Diocese of Atlanta.

Finally, he read to the congregation the four-point resolution of the Vestry. In summary, the points were:

1. Apostles terminate all relations with the Episcopal Diocese of Atlanta.
2. Apostles retain its belief and commitment to the Scriptures and to Anglican orthodoxy.
3. Apostles transfer its members and property to a new church corporation.
4. Apostles call on the leadership of the Diocese of Atlanta and the Episcopal Church to return to the faith of the scriptures.

Once he had finished reading the resolution, Gil Meredith (1$^{st}$ Rector's Warden) made the motion to withdraw from the Diocese, and Gene Hall (2$^{nd}$ Rector's Warden) seconded it. Then we distributed pertinent material and copies of the resolution.

I gave the congregation an opportunity to respond. Naturally, it was a highly emotional time for almost everyone. While the congregation debated, people started to clap for those they supported. A definite and vocal, but extremely small, group argued for us to stay. "We have to remain and fight from within," they asserted.

However, it was evident that the majority was saying, "Let's get out."

After an hour of debate, it was obvious that everything had been said. I asked if they were ready to vote.

Byron Attridge, the wise lawyer who was sitting on the platform with me, leaned over and whispered, "This is too sudden. Everybody needs an opportunity to express themselves."

"We need to think about it," said a voice from the congregation.

"Think about it?" someone answered. "We've been talking about these issues for months."

I broke in and said, "Look, I'm leaving. The Vestry is leaving. That means that Apostles' leadership is leaving. We really have no choice but to vote today. We can vote to leave as The Church of The Apostles or we can split into two factions, and the leadership will go with me to start a new congregation. That's the choice as I see it."

Actually, I don't think there was ever a question of two churches. Finally, everyone agreed that the time to vote had come. So far as we could tell, about 600 members voted. Five or six people said, "No," quite loudly, but everyone else yelled, "Yes!"

It was settled.

In our eyes, we were now independent.

Yet, as I heard the vote, my emotions were conflicted. I believed it was the right thing for us to do. In fact, I was convinced it was the only thing we could do and maintain a clear conscience with God. But there was heaviness, too. My wife was a lifelong Anglican. I had been trained in the Anglican Church. That had been my place of spiritual identification for 20 years. Now I was cutting myself off from that rich heritage. But I was certain then, and I am certain now, that we were the ones who were staying with the rich biblical-Anglican heritage and it was the Episcopal Church that left.

I felt a keen sense of loss, as if I had just witnessed the death of a person I had loved dearly.

The next day, I informed the Bishop officially of our action, but he already knew.

"Yes," he said, "I've already had some phone calls."

Although the call to the Bishop was purely a formal step on my part, it was still difficult to do. I had been ordained in the Anglican Church of Australia, and I had planned to remain in fellowship with the Episcopal Church of the United States for the rest of my life. Now it was settled; the denomination and I had parted ways.

\*\*\*

The October 14, 1991, edition of the *Atlanta Constitution* ran an article with the headline: "Church of The Apostles Secedes." The reporter, Gayle White, did a fine job of summarizing the vote:

> The 760-member Church of The Apostles, one of metro Atlanta's fastest-growing congregations, on Sunday, pulled out of the Episcopal Church. Members voted, overwhelmingly to sever ties with the Diocese of Atlanta and the national denomination's weakening moral stance.

The article closed with a statement by Bishop Allan: "It is my feeling that the inclusion and acceptance of such a wide diversity

of people and viewpoints in our church made it impossible for The
Church of The Apostles to continue its walk with us." He also
said: "The pastor and congregation will continue to be in my
prayers, and I wish them the best in their mission and ministry."

We immediately lost one member. A few others left within six
weeks. I understood why they left and I was able to say, "God
bless." However, their departure saddened me. Although I knew it
would not be possible for every member to go with us, I had
prayed that whatever action we took, it would be done with
unanimity.

All together we lost 25 people through our decision. However,
we added 200 new members the following year. Even though we
were independent, we were the same people with the same beliefs.
We did not change our style of worship. We were still The Church
of The Apostles. No one would have detected that we were any
different after October 13 than we had been the previous four
years.

We made only one important change: we now called ourselves
an Evangelical Anglican Congregation.

***

A few weeks later, we received a copy of the formal
recommendation from the Diocese's Standing Committee to
Bishop Allan. They recommended that the relationship between
The Church of The Apostles and the Episcopal Diocese of Atlanta
"be formally severed."

In a second paragraph, they recommended that I "be prohibited
from officiating as a Presbyter in the Diocese for six months." The
letter went on to state that in the event that I did not return to the
Doctrine, Discipline, and Worship of the Episcopal Church within
that time, they would recommend the implementation of Title IV,
Canon 10, Section 2. That was their way of threatening to defrock

me. In the Episcopal Church, to defrock me meant they would ask for me to return my robe and my certificate of ordination, and then I would be a layman once again.[11]

The separation and independence of Apostles was now all but official. Once the Diocesan Council acted on the recommendation of the standing committee—which they did –the relationship was severed.

"It is the time for us to move on," I told our Vestry.

Now we could carry out God's vision for Apostles.

---

[11] Although I did not return within the allotted time, no further action was taken against me.

*Chapter Twenty-Three*

## A Home of Sorts

It was time to plan for a permanent home for The Church of The Apostles. Before we left the Episcopal Church, the Diocese had insisted that we obtain their permission before we located anywhere, and have their architect approve any design that we came up with. But more importantly, they insisted that The Church of The Apostles must never have more seating capacity than that of the Cathedral church, which held 1,100.

Had we stayed with the Episcopal Church that would have led us to what the Australians call a "humm dinger" of a fight. I believed we were led to have a seating capacity of around 3,000, and that we must be located in a visible, not hidden, place.

Through our departure, the Lord had been gracious to us and had saved us from wasting unnecessary time, energy, and resources. Now we were free to locate where we felt God was leading. But the freedom to settle on a location and design of a new building was not a simple freedom. Where would we find the real estate to accommodate such a vision in the most expensive area in the southeastern United States?

A consultant advised us to buy a small plot of land, around five or six acres, and dig down four floors to build a parking garage. So we attempted to do just that. In that fashionable part of the world, it seemed like a far-fetched idea. But I said, "We will give it a shot." We found a suitable plot of land, and we put down a deposit and offered a contract with a contingency on the approval of the local neighborhood association.

The neighborhood association meeting was quite an eye-opener, however. I had never imagined that such anger and venom could be directed against a plan for a church building, especially from within the buckle of the Bible Belt. Some of the things that were uttered that night, including blasphemies, caused me deep pain.

That was on a Tuesday night.

I went home and was unable to sleep. I cried to the Lord, "We want to be here to win these people to Christ, not to be an offense. Lord, you know we are desperate. You know the Lovett School Board, though being gracious for over five years, is eager for us to move out. Lord, I will fast and pray until you show us where you want us to locate."

Thursday was my normal fasting, praying, and sermon preparation day, and on that morning around 10:30, my phone rang. It was John Wise, a member who had served on the Vestry and was an active leader in The Church of The Apostles.

"I have Carter Remes with me in the car," John said, "and we're parked right in front of the old Allstate Insurance building on Northside Parkway. We both feel the Lord may want Apostles to have this building."

I was very familiar with that building. It had been vacant for more than two years. My friend, Bill Johnson, who owned the Ritz-Carlton hotel chain and would later serve as the chairman of our building committee, had it under contract to tear down to build a Ritz-Carlton. The original price was for $17 million, but when the 1990 recession hit, he renegotiated it to $14 million. I had driven past that building and thought many times that it would be a perfect location for a church. But then I would wake up from my fantasy and remind myself that it was impossible for a congregation of 800 to raise that kind of money.

When people speak of my faith, I remind them of that and many other occasions when my faith was even smaller than a mustard seed. Now, I understand that God gives us the gift of faith when He needs us to do something for Him that is humanly impossible.

But my response to John Wise back then portrayed my lack of faith. "I've thought about that building and that location so many times," I said, "but I realized it was too rich for our blood."

But John explained that with the recession and their inability to sell it, their agent had said they were flexible.

Then my Middle Eastern blood started flowing as I wondered how low we could get it for. "How flexible?" I asked.

"Why don't you come over and meet with us. We can meet with their agent and let you see it first." Then John said, "Oh, by the way, do not tell the agent who you are."

I laughed. "With a face like mine, they'll never guess that it is a church that's looking at it."

When I met them at the Allstate building, I was wearing my leather jacket and I introduced myself as Sheikh Youssef. But the agent took John aside and said, "I know who he is. He just spoke at the Urban Land Institute breakfast a few weeks ago."

So much for trying to disguise myself. We had to come clean with their agent. But it didn't matter; God would help us work out the best possible deal for all parties.

We toured the building, and I was shocked by its condition. It had been empty for two years. The roof leaked, and rainwater drained all the way to the first floor. I had to pull up my pant legs to avoid getting wet in the two-inch-deep puddles. A naked wire held up a low light bulb in the middle of the room. The back parking lot had been used for drug-dealing and prostitution, and I could only imagine what really went on in that dark, empty place. Fortunately for us, all the tawdriness of the location and building created two favorable conditions for us: the owner was anxious to sell, and the neighbors were desperate to support any kind of development on that location.

I took individual members of the Board of Trustees and showed them the building, and then some of the Vestry members. The reaction varied from, "What in the world are you thinking?" to, "Well, it has possibilities."

Then the negotiation started in earnest. When we got to $12 million, Allstate said they could not go any lower than that.

"Great," I said.

Upon hearing my response, the treasurer of our board, Sam Ayoub, asked me, "Are you crazy? Where will you get that kind of money?"

Sam had served for years as CFO for Coca-Cola. He was also from Egypt like me, and I reminded him that we were both from a country where agreement did not mean the end of negotiation.

So I proposed that we would buy the building for $12 million if Allstate would donate $3 million to The Foundation of Holy Apostles.

Then Sam said, "Oh, I can live with that."

Once Allstate agreed, Sam negotiated an even more favorable payment arrangement, in addition to removing all of the asbestos in the building at their cost.

God then brought to us a fine new member who had a wealth of experience in developing and renovating high-rises. Billy Ivy did a remarkable job turning that tawdry, 100,000 square foot building into a sanctuary and multiple classrooms.

Finally, on Palm Sunday 1993, we moved into our new home. It was quite a celebration. A celebration of God. His faithfulness. His guidance. His overruling of my lack of faith. His leading of our steps. His protecting us from many pitfalls.

To Him alone belonged all the praise.

*Chapter Twenty-Four*

## Leading The Way

Once we became unshackled from the Episcopal bonds, we were free in every way.

Free to focus our Vestry time on prayer and planning for future evangelism.

Free to use our resources for biblical and missionary causes.

Free to build a church without going through the denominational bureaucracy for approval.

Free to seek to please the Lord alone and seek to trust and obey Him.

Free to build a ministry team who was truly called of God, regardless of their denominational affiliation.

Free to be the church of Jesus Christ, pure and simple, without the chain of hollow and pharisaic rituals.

But that freedom brought with it other challenges. Now that we were free to pursue our own vision, we had to make sure we stayed focused on it. Sometimes people joined Apostles for the purpose of changing our vision, or to put it in their words, "To make us better." The alternative directions those members advocated ranged from a charismatic tendency toward speaking in tongues, to turning us into a pure social welfare agency, and nearly everything in between.

But the members of the Vestry stood strong. Every time we faced one of those challenges, they immediately closed ranks around me and ensured that we looked neither to the right nor to the left, but upward in trusting and obeying God's global vision for us.

In one case, however, someone suggested a new idea that I rejected at first, but later reconsidered.

One year after Apostles opened its doors, my friend, Bill, kept talking to me about starting a radio ministry. But I had several problems with the idea. First, we did not have the level of members or resources necessary to start such a ministry. Second, I felt strongly that there were many fine radio ministries already on the air. And third, my time as the only pastor on staff did not afford me the luxury of the extra time needed for such a ministry.

But Bill would not give up. He believed that radio listeners were used to hearing the gospel and biblical teaching from Baptists, Evangelicals, and Pentecostals, but to hear sound biblical teaching from an Episcopalian would be something new and exciting.

I granted him that. But still, the prematurity of such a ministry made me uneasy. Furthermore, I wanted to focus on world evangelism, not just having a media ministry here in America.

But as God had done many times before, he was once again working and speaking to me through others. The vision for a radio ministry grew on me, but I still didn't know if the idea was from God or just from a well-meaning friend who had a wonderful plan for my life.

For several years, I avoided the vision of a radio ministry until God finally broke through. During prayer, I felt him pushing me to do it. What God understood, but I couldn't see at the time, was that

He would use a radio program to fulfill His global evangelical vision for The Church of The Apostles.

I decided to give it a try. Through the help of a friend who was a minister of music, I recorded 60-second spots and was able to get them broadcast on Peach FM in Atlanta.

Three years after my friend first mentioned that idea, we had started the radio ministry that today is known as Leading The Way.

*** 

Soon we were able to get my messages broadcast on a handful of radio stations in Atlanta and the Southeast. Among those was a radio station in the Raleigh/Durham/Cary area of North Carolina. Cary happened to be the headquarters for Trans World Radio (TWR), an organization I was very familiar with. I had grown up listening to TWR Radio Monte Carlo.

One of their executives, Bill Damick, listened to my messages and saw an opportunity. More than once, he called Joe Emmett— Leading The Way's Executive Director and first full-time employee—with a simple request: "I feel led to approach you to consider translating and broadcasting Michael's radio messages into the Arab-speaking world."

My immediate response was, "No way."

Again, I felt like this new idea was somebody else's vision and not from God. I had experienced enough pain in my life by following the plans of man and not God that I never wanted to do that again. I only wanted to follow His perfect will and to experience the incomparable joy of knowing I was trusting and obeying God, of knowing that I was following His GPS. So I was typically cautious. I wouldn't immediately follow a new road if I wasn't sure about God's involvement.

But I had two other reasons for saying no to TWR's invitation. First, I understood enough about languages to know that literal translations of my sermons preached in the US would only make sense to a few mature Christians in the Middle East. My heart wanted to focus on explaining the gospel to those who had a totally confused picture of it. Second, I felt the dreaded limitation of time and money.

But after Bill Damick called again, I found myself on my knees asking, "Lord, am I missing something? Am I wrong in waiting for a better time? Am I fearful of the sacrifices of time and resources that I will have to make?"

A short time later I read some statistics about the Middle East from the BBC. The bottom line of those statistics were as follows:

Seventy-five percent of the population of the region is under 15 years old.

And they all want to learn English.

When I read that, I felt the Lord say, "Here's the answer to your reluctance to broadcast into the Arabic-speaking world."

So I went to Joe Emmett with an idea. I asked him to call Bill Damick and propose a program where I prepared culturally relevant messages, then sat in a studio with a translator, spoke one sentence in English, and had the translator speak that same sentence in Arabic. That way listeners could learn English, hear the gospel explained, and have their questions answered at the same time.

But when TWR ran that concept by the folks who operated the Arabic division in Monte Carlo, they gave it a thumbs-down. Although part of me was relieved—I did not cherish the thought of all that preparation and time it would take—part of me was disappointed.

"Well, I have done my part," I said to Joe. "Obviously God is not in this."

But that perception didn't last very long. About six weeks later, Bill Damick called back. "The folks in Monte Carlo decided to give it a shot. Just broadcast a few programs and we'll see what happens."

The response was phenomenal. After the first few broadcasts, hundreds of letters poured in to the Egyptian office of TWR. College professors and high school teachers wrote that they were asking their English language students to listen to the program as part of their class assignments.

Still, the growth in funding for Leading The Way was slow at first. Sometimes, I wondered if we had started too soon and moved ahead of God's timing. The road was not always smooth. But as word began to spread about our dual language program, requests came from other media outlets in Asia and elsewhere. We launched broadcasts in Mandarin, Indonesian, Turkish, and Persian. Leading The Way had taken off, and eventually, the funding came.

Today, we broadcast in 20 of the world's most spoken languages, covering nearly 4 billion people. It has been an amazing accomplishment, but I cringe every time someone gives the credit to me. They do not understand that all I did was trust and obey— reluctantly at that.

\*\*\*

Despite the fast growth of Leading The Way, the global vision for The Church of The Apostles had yet to make its most dramatic turn—a turn that no one could've predicted, including me.

For many years, I had half-seriously said, "I will never go on television. I have a face for radio." My impression of Christian television was that to hold people's attention you had to be half-comedian, half-gymnast. I didn't believe Christian television audiences would respond to the serious-minded preaching of the word of God.[12]

My wife, on the other hand, used to say, "You will be on television over my dead body." She had a slightly different reasoning from mine. She felt the over-exposure that television created actually reduced the effectiveness of a ministry.

Well, what happened on a Friday morning in October 1999 would make us both eat our words.

It was about 10 a.m. when Brenda Williams, my administrative assistant, told me that Ben Haden was on the phone. Ben Haden was the Senior Pastor of First Presbyterian Church of Chattanooga for 23 years, and he was a pioneer in Christian radio and television. I said to put him through right away.

One Sunday earlier that year, Ben had attended worship at Apostles. When I spotted him afterward in the receiving line, I left my place up front and pulled him out of line and greeted him warmly. He was choked up at first and could not talk. But then he said, "You will hear from me later."

When I got on the phone, Ben said in his typical humility, "This is Ben Haden. Does the name mean anything to you?"

"Of course, Ben. You were here a few months ago. Furthermore, I have followed and admired your ministry and integrity for many years."

He immediately said, "I need to see you."

"Well, let me check my calendar—"

"You don't understand. I'm in the car and passing Dalton, Georgia, on my way to see you now."

---

[12] A few years after the television ministry started, I felt vindicated in that opinion when a Hollywood consultant told me that I needed to "lighten up."

"No problem, Ben. Come on in." I immediately scrambled to reschedule my lunch appointment and arranged to have lunch provided for Ben and me.

When Ben arrived, he again was emotional. Being an emotional man myself, I empathized with his state and thought he must be facing a crisis. I felt honored that he would come and see me about it. But it turned out to be a crisis of a different kind.

"I won't prolong this. I want to get to the point of why I'm here. For the past two and a half years, the Lord has been telling me to give you my radio and television ministry, Change Lives. Every time I resisted or thought of somebody else, the Lord kept putting your name in front of me."

I tried to lighten up the situation by attempting a joke, but Ben didn't laugh. Then I told him how Elizabeth had said for years that I would be on television "over her dead body." At that, Ben got up without touching his lunch. "That's your problem. I have delivered the message."

As he sped toward the door, I ran after him. I walked to his car with him and said, "I really need time to pray about this. I need to be sure this is what the Lord wants me to do."

After Ben left, I immediately walked into the office of my assistant, Dana Blackwood. Dana represented me on the building committee for the new sanctuary we were building. Those who knew Dana knew he was a jack-of-all-trades. He was a fantastic singer, and he understood buildings, wires, and electronics. He had once worked in a church with a mega-television ministry before it went defunct because of moral failure, so he understood my reluctance about television.

When Dana saw the panic on my face, he asked me what was wrong. I told him what Ben had said. Then I asked, "If this is of the Lord, could we film without turning the sanctuary into a television studio?" I could never preach where cameramen were running around all the time. It would be too distracting, plus I just wanted to preach to the flock, not to the camera. If a broadcast of my normal preaching could be used to bless others, then that was well and good.

Dana said the new sanctuary was already equipped with conduits through which wires could be run, and it wasn't too late to have those conduits utilized for robotic cameras.

And once again, the rest was history. Thanks to Ben's obedience and Dana's know-how, The Church of The Apostles was soon on the air. God was continuing to fulfill His global vision for our church. Eventually, we would have our own television channel dedicated to the preaching of the gospel 24/7.

Today, THE KINGDOM SAT televises the gospel message into 140 million homes in the Arabic-speaking world and in Europe and is expanding into many other parts of the world. We host many wonderful teachers, evangelists, and apologists—both Arabic and English speakers. But to start and grow the television ministry, we had to rely on the infrastructure put in place by Leading The Way. The trust and obedience needed to start that radio ministry led to further obedience in regards to THE KINGDOM SAT.

The story of The Church of The Apostles, of Leading The Way, and of THE KINGDOM SAT is a story about God and His faithfulness. It is a story about His search for people who are willing to trust and obey.

If you are going through a time of questioning or uncertainty, let me encourage you. Although God does not deal with two people in the same way, His character is unchangeable. He is still looking for those who will say, "I will go anywhere, do anything, as long as I know that You are in it."

*Chapter Twenty-Five*

## A Sanctuary for the Glory of God

Every year during my talk at our annual congregational meeting, I would quip, "Wouldn't it be great to have a new building in front of this one to hide its ugliness?" Most everyone would politely laugh; after all, they did not want to embarrass their pastor. But some were not laughing. Among them were members of the Board of Trustees who had often talked seriously about a new sanctuary.

There was a sweet unity when, once a year, the trustees and the members of the Vestry would get together for a few hours to pray and talk about a building. There was, and continues to be, a mutual respect and admiration between the two bodies. Back then, the questions were: When will we build a new sanctuary? And what type of building do we envision?

Some pastors I knew had split their churches over a building program, and I was adamant that Apostles would not experience that. Fresh in my mind was a story of a pastor who demanded a very exquisite and expensive building. He got his church into such debt, that they not only split, and many left, but he had to resign from the church he had founded.

That church's interim pastor had invited me to speak on the heel of those disastrous events, and I had never experienced such a dejected and depressed congregation. During the four-hour drive back to Atlanta, I kept saying to my wife, "By God's grace, power, and strength that will never happen at Apostles."

As is often the case, people tend to go to extremes. And to an extreme I went. I announced to the leadership that I believed our new building should be very simple. Little did I know that God had already laid the opposite vision on the heart of the man who later became Chairman of the Board of Trustees, Hank McCamish. His vision was from God; mine was from fear and a reaction to another's experience.

When we finally decided that we needed the additional worship space, Hank brought up three points to the Board of Trustees. First, he asked, "Why should we build something for God that is less than the homes we have built for ourselves?" Second, he reminded the board that we would never have a second chance to do this right. And finally, he said, "God did not place this church in a poor area. If He had, it would be appropriate to build a sanctuary that respected our limited resources. Instead, He placed us in a wealthy area, and He expects us to present something for His glory as part of our testimony."

The board took Hank's words to heart and agreed with them. Our architect, Bill Chegwidden, also caught hold of the vision. He wanted something that would be strikingly visible from I-75, the second busiest highway in the country, and the design became very personal to him.

Sometimes pastors get carried away in thinking that, just because God gave them a vision for the overall church, they have God's vision in every aspect of the church. That's a big mistake.

The Lord has always been gracious to me, and He often rebukes me quickly when I have not heard His voice or when I push for a personal preference. Now that I am older, I sometimes tell our leadership and ministry team, "I really do not know the mind of the Holy Spirit on this, but I am ready to hear from others who do."

When people try to give me credit for how magnificent Apostles' building is today, I stop them dead in their tracks. "If it had been up to me, this would be a very basic building." But Hank had caught God's vision, and he challenged the other trustees to catch the vision, too. Over the years, God has used Hank in many ways, not least of all in championing the building overlooking Interstate 75, known irreverently to some as The Church of Our Lady of 75.

* * *

My friendship with Hank and Margaret McCamish went back to 1977, when I had the pleasure of sitting next to them at a dinner hosted by Dr. John Haggai and the Haggai Institute.[13] Then, when we moved to Atlanta in January 1979, our friendship developed and grew. Between 1989 and 2005, Hank, Margaret, Elizabeth and I travelled overseas numerous times and our bond of friendship deepened. The McCamishes belonged to another church until 1995, but our friendship was as strong as ever.

Early in the morning on Good Friday 1993, Hank called me to discuss a personal matter. We had just moved into the old Allstate Insurance building, now renovated into our church. "The furniture has not yet been set in my office," I said to Hank, "but let's meet there anyway." When we got to my office, we sat on boxes of books. Hank was very emotional as he started to share his personal challenge. So I said, "Before we get to talking about this challenge, let me tell you a secret. For over ten years I have prayed for you and Margaret."

---

[13] Hank was Chairman of the Board for the Haggai Institute that year.

179

I shared that my prayer for him was to come into a deeper commitment to Christ. Already Hank and Margaret had been some of the most generous people I knew. By Hank's own testimony (which he gave to 300 men a year later), for 60 years he had confused being a churchman and a generous giver with what it meant to be born-again.

As we knelt on the bare floor that Good Friday morning, Hank committed his life and resources completely to the Lord.

As a pastor I have seen numerous dedications and rededications, and sometimes very little comes from them. But not with Hank. He immediately put shoe leather on his dedication, and his generosity turned into a flood gate of total giving.

\*\*\*

One area where Hank made a major impact was in our Leading The Way ministry. Although the demand for our broadcasts had grown quickly during the first two years, we often lacked the funds we needed. So with a heavy heart, I called the board together in 1992 and asked them to help me close the ministry and pay off our bills. I hoped that we could restart again later when we had more resources and personnel.

A group of very sympathetic friends made up the board for Leading The Way, and they understood how I felt and said they would help me close the ministry. All of them agreed, except one—the Chairman, Hank McCamish.

Hank asked two simple questions: "Did God raise up this ministry? And is it having an impact?"

The answer to both was yes.

"Then this vote is totally out of place," he said.

Today, Leading The Way is broadcasted more than 3,800 times a day and impacts tens of millions of lives. Humanly speaking, that would not have happened if not for the foresight of Hank McCamish.

Despite the hundreds of ways God has used him through numerous ministries, he hates accolades or even acknowledgements. Once, he threatened to end our friendship if I told people how God had really used him. So I shall wait until the Lord takes him to glory.

In 2005, Hank began to suffer from Parkinson's disease. Although he is incapacitated and cannot speak, he is still adamant that we do not put his name on any building. We would like to do that so we can glorify God's faithfulness to him, but he remains opposed to any public recognition.

Whenever you see Hank McCamish's name on any building in the city of Atlanta, you can be assured that he was not consulted or told about it beforehand.

I have had the privilege of knowing some very good stewards in my lifetime, but none a more joyful giver and none more intentional about their giving than Hank McCamish. For most people, stewardship is ten percent. To Hank, it was all of it. But God is no man's debtor, and the more Hank gave, the more God piled back to him.

The Lord wants to see His work on earth accomplished, so He looks for the Hank McCamishes of this world. People who see themselves not as a reservoir, but as a channel. God keeps giving to them, so they may keep on giving it back to Him.

If Christians would begin to comprehend that simple principle, we could have evangelized the world three times over. But the work of God often languishes because many Christians are chincy with God, nickel-and-diming Him instead of being ecstatic givers.

\*\*\*

The Church of The Apostles was blessed, however, with many ecstatic givers. Although the design of our structure became anything but simple, we still kept our fundraising efforts very simple. In fact, they were almost non-existent.

We did not have a building campaign. I did not get in the pulpit each Sunday and talk about how much money we needed to raise for the sanctuary. We did not put out a big thermostat sign and fill in the red area as the contributions came in. We did not even need to borrow money and get into complex financial arrangements. We just prayed. And God did the rest.

Visitors to Apostles would hear someone talking about a new sanctuary, and they would be shocked to learn there was no organized effort to raise money. "You don't have a campaign?" they would ask incredulously.

I would raise the topic of the building funds about once every six months just to tell the congregation, "Here is what God is doing . . . ." However, we did not want fundraising to distract us from worship and serving God. I had a laser-beam focus on our vision, and our attention did not need to be diverted toward a building. As people gave money, we thanked God and the donors, and then we set the money aside.

Once we settled on the location and style of the building, we turned to William B. Johnson to lead the building development. Bill had developed many hotels—some Marriotts, some Holiday Inns—before he developed the trend-setting hotel chain The Ritz-Carlton (with the help of some colleagues such as Horst Schulze, the first president of The Ritz-Carlton Hotels and also a member of Apostles).

Bill was renowned for his passionate pursuit of excellence, and we were blessed to have him as a trustee and the Chairman of the Sanctuary Building Committee. As expected, Bill attacked this project with passion and commitment. For nearly two years he prodded, encouraged, pulled, and pushed, to ensure that we would celebrate Christmas Eve in the new sanctuary.

Although I did not always feel comfortable with the elaborate design, I tried to submit to the authority of others when they took responsibility for their decisions and when their decisions reflected the will of God. So I was glad to go along for the ride. But sometimes, I was even more than glad.

The gothic style of the sanctuary inspired me (it would soon become one of the most prominent landmarks in Atlanta). And the interior was warm and vibrant—with slate floors, stained glass windows, traditional pews, and light-reflecting colors. As the construction started to take shape, I would walk through the sanctuary and then sit on the bare concrete floor in the balcony. A feeling of awe would overcome me. "You are a marvelous God," I would say, over and over again. The beauty of the place seemed to shout our praises to the Lord on our behalf.

Our first service in the new sanctuary was on Christmas Eve 2000. Bill Johnson was there until midnight the night before, coordinating the lighting installation crews, the wiring crews, and the pew crews. It was a mad dash to the finish. Last minute things were still being completed until 4:00 p.m. the next day. Then the congregation came at 5:00 p.m., and we celebrated the birth of our new worship home along with the birth of our Savior.

Today, I am still moved to praise God when I walk inside the sanctuary. And visitors are drawn to Apostles because they drive by it on the highway and wonder what goes on inside such a dramatic structure. Once inside, they meet people who are warm and friendly, and they hear the life-saving gospel of Jesus Christ.

Our new building was important to praise God and bring new people to hear the good news. The details of how it was built, its structure and appearance, every aspect, gave glory to God and thanked Him for the faithfulness of Hank McCamish.

* * *

Although our belief that we needed a larger sanctuary was right on the mark, we had not considered that our children's ministry would explode as a result of a new building and ample parking spaces. Thus, we now needed more space for the children's ministry.

After a great deal of deliberation, we settled on demolishing the existing small chapel and building a more versatile chapel and fellowship center (which we called "The Commons"), plus a five-story addition above the chapel with adequate classrooms for both children and adults.

Dana Blackwood once again represented me on the building committee (as he had with the sanctuary) with his usual commonsense knowledge. For the construction, we turned to Jim Caswell, another man with a wealth of experience from being a major developer in the United States and around the world.

Jim is a unique human being and a very dear brother. I fondly refer to his demeanor as "quiet eloquence," because although he was a quiet man, whenever he opened his mouth, he spoke volumes in few words. Jim and Carolyn Caswell had arrived at Apostles after watching how their beloved Presbyterian Church was fast joining the Episcopal Church in abandoning the word of God as their foundational truth. They visited Apostles for a while, but immediately after joining, they became pillars of our church.

When Jim was tapped to head up the building of the new educational tower, it was clear that there would be very little drama—only action and quality. Jim and his committee turned to the Van Winkle Construction Company, who had built the sanctuary under budget and ahead of time. Once again, that class act of a company did it again in building the ministry tower.

Before we started construction on the new educational tower, the leadership of Apostles gave the congregation a challenge. For every dollar we spent on the building, we would give one dollar to global evangelism. It was an inspiration to watch the faithful congregation of The Church of The Apostles take up that challenge and give even more than was needed.

The building was completed in November 2004, and we once again celebrated God's faithfulness and the vision and generosity of the people of Apostles. We had come a long way from that first gathering at the Waverly Hotel.

*Chapter Twenty-Six*

## The People of Apostles

During our first days, some people had come to Apostles not knowing exactly what to expect. But the Holy Spirit had moved within them. Tears fell down their faces. They raised their hands to commit their lives to Christ. They met me in my office after the service to learn more about their Savior. Now with the sanctuary and the education tower completed, a lot had changed. But one thing remained the same: God was still at work among us— drawing us in and sending us out.

At The Church of The Apostles, our mission has been to serve God by helping people learn about the Lord and grow in a deeper relationship with Him. People come to the Lord through many avenues, such as worshiping Him, studying the Bible, dealing with grief, dealing with sin, and watching a program on TV. We have sought to serve God in as many avenues as possible.

There have been thousands of personal testimonies connected with The Church of The Apostles. Through our 25 years, the people of Apostles have shared their testimonies during worship, Sunday school, small group gatherings, and on the Internet. Their stories have shown the Lord at work. They have inspired non-believers to turn toward the Lord, while encouraging believers to seek an ever closer relationship with Him.

For that reason, one of the best ways to show God's work at Apostles is to share a few of those testimonies. Our Father has offered each of us a remarkable peace treaty through His Son, Jesus Christ. May these stories remind us of how the Lord reaches out to each of us as well.[14]

*** 

### Patrick Rodgers
*Learning about Christ through Bible Study*

Patrick Rodgers grew up on a farm in Christiana, Jamaica. They raised rabbits for protein, grew bananas and citrus fruits, and ran a dairy operation. Patrick would get up early in the morning to milk the cows, tie up the goats, and feed the rabbits.

They had everything they needed, and Patrick lived a fun, carefree existence. It was a safe island at the time, and when he wasn't doing chores, he spent a lot of time walking around and riding his bicycle. Patrick's parents were divorced, and his father wasn't around much. But he really didn't miss him; Patrick's mother was a loving and attentive woman, and she provided whatever he needed.

After Patrick grew up, he fell in love with Marjorie at a moonlight picnic. Patrick had been invited to join the group picnic because he was the only person in the area to own a portable phonograph. Patrick and Marjorie got married and started a family as Patrick's career took off. He worked hard, and eventually, he served as the marketing director for the island's largest brewery, head of the Airports Authority, and Chairman of the Board for the University Hospital of the West Indies.

---

[14] Most of these testimonies were originally given by video and currently can be found on our website. A longer version of Gayle York's testimony was originally posted on our blog and currently can be found there also.

Marjorie wanted their children to grow up in the church, so she took them to church regularly. But Patrick often went to the golf course instead. His work was his focus and passion, and he poured his energy into it. God was not a factor in any of the family decision-making that involved Patrick. He was comfortable and didn't worry himself with God.

But then things started to change. A new government, headed by Michael Manley, had taken over in Jamaica, and they had decided to move the country toward communism. As a businessman, Patrick knew he had done everything he could do in Jamaica. So he decided to move his family to the United States.

Patrick's now-grown daughter, Karyn, says, "Looking back on it, I believe that was the beginning of God drawing us out of our Egypt, where everything was comfortable."

The Rodgers family came to Atlanta where Patrick started an import/export business. Later he bought Mathis Dairy, and then he went into the real estate development business. Karyn remembers that when she was in college and studying late at night, her father was always up working. "Two in the morning, four in the morning. He was always working it seemed. Numbers, figuring out stuff, that was his security."

Patrick occasionally went to church with his family, but he felt like no one really explained the Bible well. He didn't understand it, and he didn't pursue any greater knowledge. Patrick felt that he could "worship God on the golf course," so he continued to spend many of his Sunday mornings there. His Sundays were for living a carefree life like he had done as a child in Jamaica.

Then one Sunday, Marjorie attended The Church of the Apostles, and she knew she had found a new church home. She started taking the children there and attending regularly.

Years passed. The children grew up, and Patrick grew older. But he still avoided God. Then one Sunday at Apostles, we talked about the idols in our lives, and Karyn realized that her dad was an idol to her. She loved him, but he was not a godly man. She wrestled with the fear that he would go to hell if he died. So she cried out to the Lord, "Please give my dad mercy. Please give him enough time for him to know salvation."

For 74 years, Patrick had never thought of God as someone real. "I thought of him as some sort of myth." But his family prevailed upon him to join the church, and he finally agreed. When he went through the membership process, one of our leaders, J.C. Poole, offered to lead him in a one-on-one Bible study for six weeks.

Patrick bonded easily with J.C., and he found himself absorbing everything he said. Patrick detected a sincerity in him, and a real love for Christ that influenced Patrick's thinking. Patrick felt free to ask a lot of questions, which he did.

One of those questions was, "If God is real, why can't we go to him directly?"

J.C. explained that we can never be good enough to go to God, that's why He sent his son. J.C. drew on the board a diagram that showed the chasm between God and us, and how the cross filled that gap. At that moment, a light bulb came on for Patrick.

"I started to think about Christ as my friend, as someone I could approach and talk to."

J.C.'s instruction gave Patrick the answers he needed. What had never been explained adequately before was now clear. During week three, J.C. taught a lesson on having a relationship with Christ. Following the lesson, he said a prayer that asked for a growing relationship with the Lord. When Patrick heard the prayer, he said, "I want to pray that." So he did. He had finally accepted the Lord.

Patrick's life was changed on that day. He put God first, not his work. Now he says, "There is nothing I can think of that is greater than accepting Jesus Christ as your savior," he says. "It has brought me great, great joy."

***

*Liza Stepat*
*Developing a Relationship with the Lord through STS*

Liza grew up in a very loving family, and her parents taught her about God from the start. She was very involved in the youth group at Apostles. She felt like she knew all the answers and could talk easily about Jesus. But in reality, Liza says that she was focused more on herself. She wanted to look good, to be perceived as "the best Christian."

Then, during the summer before 7th grade, her family moved to Woodstock, Georgia. Liza was depressed during that time; they had left Apostles, and she had left all her friends, everything she had known. Without that support system, doubts about her faith crept in. *What do I really believe?* she wondered.

One day she went to lunch with a friend, and her friend talked about the gospel and how Jesus came and died for us. But Liza's heart was troubled. *I know all this,* she thought. *What am I missing?*

But fortunately Liza's time away from Apostles didn't last long. Her family felt the Lord calling them back despite the distance. So they returned, and Liza immediately got involved in the STS (Student to Student) Ministry. Through STS, Liza learned that God wants to have a relationship with us. That was the part she had been missing.

191

Brian Skaggs, the Director of STS, says that he often sees teenagers struggling with false identities. "Maybe their identity is wrapped up in something they're trying to be. But the truth is, when the gospel transforms our lives, we are a new creation."

STS does not put on a big show for students so they can be entertained. Instead, we want them to go deep, to develop a deep relationship with Christ. And then, as Christ transforms them, we want them to go out into the world and be used by the Lord.

One day she said to God, "Okay, I believe what you're saying is true, and you're real, and you love me and want a relationship with me." On that day, her faith came alive. Liza asked God to give her faith to believe that His word is true, and through that faith, to grow closer to Him and have a blessed and full life.

"I think our generation sometimes thinks they can fool God," she says. "But you miss the whole point when you just go to church to check that box." Liza had learned that a relationship with God permeated every facet of life. "It's more than just a hobby. It's a lifestyle."

Later, Liza traveled to Africa with a group of teenagers from Apostles. During one part of their trip, the group worked around the clock to create a skit to present to a couple of hundred Zimbabwean teenagers. Because of the language barrier, they decided to present a silent skit where the movements alone told the story. But when they performed it, the Zimbabwean audience started laughing. They didn't understand what was happening.

When the skit was over, however, Liza suddenly felt moved to verbally explain what had been going on. Through a translator, Liza explained the skit, step by step. Those couple of hundred Zimbabwean teenagers went from laughing to being fixated on the gospel. "It was like my mouth just opened and words just came out that weren't mine. I wasn't even thinking. It was completely the Holy Spirit taking over."

Today, Liza mentors the younger girls at Apostles, sharing the importance of a relationship with Jesus Christ. But she also talks to people outside the church. For instance, Liza works at a fast food restaurant, and one day she was talking with her boss about God. Her boss said, "I believe in God, so I think I'm going to heaven."

But the more they talked, Liza realized that her boss didn't know anything about having an actual relationship with the Lord. Since then, Liza has been sharing the gospel with her and emphasizing the importance of having that relationship.

Liza believes God wants to use her time in high school to grow her. She needs to prepare for the life God has planned for her. "So when he has a task for me and says, 'I want you to go there,' I'm equipped."

***

*Kayla Cason*
*Taking Children's Ministry into the Mission Field*

Kayla always had a passion for kids. Even as a little girl, she loved taking care of other little children and spending time with them. Early on, she felt God calling her to be a teacher.

But after she became a teacher in a public school, she felt called to not only teach academics to the children, but to teach them about Jesus. At Apostles, we have often talked about how to use our spiritual gifts to share the gospel. That had led Kayla to pray and read the scriptures in an effort to discern how she could best help her students.

Then, before school started in August, her principal announced that if any teachers had a special interest they wanted to expose the students to, something they could share with the students before or after school, then they could run it by her and she would consider it.

So Kayla approached her principal and said she wanted to start a club to teach the children about Christ. And to Kayla's delight, her principal said yes.

Although Kayla taught in a public school, she was legally free to teach about Christ as long as it was in a club setting and open to the entire school. Kayla immediately got in touch with Connie Musselman, the Director of Children's Ministry at Apostles, and Connie offered to provide Bibles and other resources for the new club.

The club started with the beginning of the school year. On the first day, four kids attended. But they told their siblings and other friends about it, and it quickly grew until 20-25 were coming consistently.

The children were committed because they had to come in early to attend the club. "They were so excited," Kayla says. Week after week, "they came in with smiling faces and their Bibles, and they were very eager to learn about Christ."

Later that year, Connie mentioned to Kayla that Apostles would love to have the children attend our Vacation Bible School that summer. Kayla thought it was a great idea. The only issue was that the church was forty miles away from the school, and Kayla drove a 5-passenger sedan. But she decided to see how many kids would like to go and then figure things out from there.

A good friend and fellow teacher had a 15-passenger van and offered to swap vehicles for the week. Then when Kayla announced the plans for Vacation Bible School, all the children said they wanted to go. Eventually, fifteen students signed up.

The kids loved attending our Bible school. The children would sing the songs with Kayla in the van on the way home each day, and they shared them with their family and friends. One mom sent Kayla a video of her daughter and another friend singing one of the VBS songs. The mom was so appreciative, and it touched Kayla's heart.

It was a wonderful experience for everyone, including Kayla. She had wanted to teach the kids about the Lord, and in the past, she did the best she could, often in a disguised way. "But I was so tired of that," she says. "I wanted to openly express my faith with these kids."

She didn't know what they faced at home. "From what I hear, it's not good things. They don't go to church, and you can just look at their eyes; they're sad. They want more."

The world can be a difficult place, and children aren't immune from facing those difficulties. But Kayla wanted to bring them joy. She wanted them to know "there's a Savior and He loves you and He wants you to know that."

At Apostles, we've talked about looking at our lives as a mission field. And Kayla sees it that way. She goes into the public school environment every day where she says people are afraid to speak about God and show His love. "But if you're sold out to God, nothing should intimidate you," she says. "If you're a Christian, you'll have that desire to share it with others."

Today, Kayla continues to share the gospel through her club. She wants to see her students being disciples. She wants to "equip them, so they can see that they can also go out and talk to others about the Lord."

***

### Bud Workmon
*Finding the Road to Healing through Living Waters*

Bud Workmon grew up on an island off the coast of Georgia. He lived a "Huckleberry Finn" childhood, spending most of the time running around barefoot, and as he says, "fishing, crabbing, shrimping, and getting into trouble."

One day, Bud and his brother were hanging out at a neighbor's house. At the house was a family who was visiting from Louisiana, including two boys and their father. Unfortunately, the three of them got into a fight with Bud and his brother. It was three against two, and one of them was an adult, so things did not go well. "We got whooped," Bud says.

They ran back home, and their dad happened to be there at the time. Bud expected his father to jump up, run over to the neighbor's house, and take revenge on the man who had beat up his boys. "That's the way we normally thought," Bud says.

Instead, his father admonished Bud and his brother for getting into the fight. He accused them of starting it.

"He didn't defend us," Bud says.

That changed how Bud thought about his life. From that day forward, he believed he would need to take care of himself. *Nobody else is going to take care of me.*

"My life was all about me," Bud says after his father didn't stand up for him. "And that ended up being my downfall."

Bud grew up on the back side of the island where people didn't have much money. But he couldn't help noticing the rich people who lived on the front side along the intercoastal waterway—people with big houses and yachts. "That was success to me," Bud says.

Wealth gave him a picture of how he wanted life to be, so as an adult, he set out to achieve that dream. Eventually, Bud started a small business with some friends. The business grew and was successful, and they ended up selling it to a major national company. Instantly, he had everything he wanted. Now he could buy the expensive boat and all the other nice things he desired.

By acquiring those things, he also hoped his wife, family, and friends would give him lots of recognition for everything he was doing for them. But when he did not get as much appreciation as he thought he deserved, he turned to people who would better value all those expensive things.

Bud cheated on his wife. He had the means to buy the appreciation of other women, and he liked how much they paid attention to him. He was now living in Atlanta, but he often wasn't there. He started traveling a lot after his company was acquired, and while on the road, he lived a life of infidelity.

But then things got even worse. One time while Bud was on a business trip in Reno, Nevada, he went to a casino to kill some time. He dropped $50 into a slot machine and hit the jackpot. That started his gambling addiction.

As he gambled, he noticed the lifestyles of the other gamblers he hung out with. They all had beautiful women with them, and people loved to hear their big-spender gambling stories. So Bud became a high-roller gambler.

During a six-year period, Bud continued to travel a lot, while living out his life of gambling and infidelity. However, his wife, Kathy, remained committed to making their marriage work. But there were times when she just threw up her hands and wanted him gone. "I relished those times," says Bud, "because I could go off and gamble and live my unfaithful lifestyle."

But there came a time when Kathy truly had enough. In 2006, Bud and she agreed to meet at their lake house in the north Georgia mountains to discuss their marriage. After they arrived, they sat down and talked. Kathy looked Bud in the eyes and said, "I release you. I don't need you anymore. I don't count on you for my happiness or for anything else. I have everything I need in Jesus Christ."

After Kathy finished talking, Bud went out on the screen porch to think. While sitting there, he noticed a small book that was sitting on the table. It was called, *God Works in the Small Things*, and Bud picked it up and started reading it. But then, all of a sudden, he put it down. Kathy's release of him had forced him to see his life clearly. He knew then that he couldn't go on living the life he had been living. He knew it was sinful, and he knew he didn't want to lose Kathy. So he prayed. "Father, I can't do this anymore. I'm done. I'm screwing up my life, and I want to give you control over it right now."

Bud wept uncontrollably for half an hour. It was a purifying experience. "I felt like I had been washed," Bud says. "Like someone had dumped water on me. I felt clean."

Bud started attending Apostles regularly with Kathy, and he joined the Living Waters group. "That's where the rubber met the road for me," Bud says. "It was *the* best thing that ever happened to me, outside of being saved."

Living Waters is a 28-week intensive study that helps people remove the blocks to intimacy with Christ by working through their wounds, sin, and baggage. Through Living Waters, Bud saw God working in other people's lives. He heard their stories of healing. "The powerful witness that occurs in that ministry is unbelievable," he says.

As a result of coming to the Lord and going through Living Waters, Bud and Kathy's marriage healed. Not only that, Bud felt good about himself. He felt a joy he had never felt before.

In a beautiful ceremony, Bud and Kathy renewed their wedding vows. "Because I was a new creation," Bud says, "we needed to get married again."

When people see Bud today, he just wants them to see the Lord. "I'm not perfect, and I do fail. But the biggest change in me is when I wake up every morning and the only thing I want to do is honor God."

***

*Deborah Lee*

*Overcoming Doubts through Worship*

Deborah's mother loved the old hymns, and she wanted her children to grow up in the church. So Deborah attended church until late in her high school years. She was baptized at 12 years old, but at the time, she didn't really understand what that meant.

As she was finishing high school, however, she gave up on Christianity. She had three very close friends, and she trusted them a lot. They were very intelligent, well-read people, and she had a lot of respect for their opinions. One day her friends sat her down to have a talk with her. "This Christianity thing is for simple-minded people," one of them said. "We believe you're smarter than this. You've got to let go of this silly story and start looking into other things."

One of those friends was Deborah's best friend growing up, and they ended up going to college together. At college, her friend took some religious studies courses and would come home and talk about them. They seemed interesting to Deborah, so she also signed up to take one.

She took a course on Buddhism, Taoism, and Confucianism, but those didn't seem to offer the right direction for her. So she took classes on Native American studies. Her father used to say they had some Cherokee in them, so that also piqued her interest. Deborah studied Zuni, Hopi, Lakota Sioux, among others.

"Thoughts of atheism have always been what I battled," Deborah says. "I was looking for answers. I was looking for proof. And I didn't see that in Christianity. It wasn't obvious to me."

199

But Native American spirituality seemed easier to grasp. It also held out the possibility of proof. A common practice among many Native American tribes was receiving visions. They would go to a quiet place, maybe up on a mountain, and there they would pray and meditate for several days. So Deborah thought, *Maybe I can receive a vision that would give me proof about God.*

After college, Deborah planned to go teach on a reservation. She went home first, however, with plans to teach there for one year and save up her money. But some personal things happened, and she never left for the reservation.

Later, she met John, and they started dating. "One of the first things I found out about him was that he was a God-centered man." John was a member of Apostles, and he took her to our church. Here, she heard an unwavering belief in God from an educated perspective, and she heard about having a personal relationship with Jesus Christ.

During that visit, Deborah says she felt like she heard truth for the first time, and "it was truth with an expectation of responsibility."

From my sermon that day, Deborah received a message that we were all responsible for our relationship with Christ, and there were no excuses for ignoring that. Deborah loved that. "Finally someone saying, 'We're not going to mix it to make people comfortable. It drew me in, and I wanted to know more."

With her skeptical mind, however, Deborah didn't feel worthy to be a Christian. But John told her, "Everybody has doubts. It's a matter of putting your faith into it."

With that encouragement, Deborah decided to fully engage herself in following Christ. But she wasn't sure how to go about it.

Soon Christmas came, and Deborah and John attended one of our Christmas Eve services. She came to the service ready to move toward Christ. She prayed, "God, put this in front of me so I will know how I'm supposed to do this."

Later during the service, I said a prayer, and Deborah felt as if I was speaking directly to her. The prayer included these words: "I pray tonight that not a single person would reject this incredible peace treaty that will, not only bring joy and contentment here and now, but forever with you." Then later in the prayer, I said to people in the congregation, "If you used to be a Christian, and you strayed, but now you're back, if your heart is here and you want to make that commitment, then join me in this prayer . . . ."

That was what Deborah was waiting to hear. It was the sign she had asked God for. She said the prayer and began her journey in relationship with Christ.

*** 

## Gayle York
### *Finding New Life through GriefShare*

Gayle York was five years old when she and her twin brother, Tim, knelt down with their mother and prayed to receive Christ. "My faith was given to me on a silver platter," she says. "I'm grateful that I never had to go looking for it." But even when faith is easily found, life is difficult. Gayle found that out at age 13 when her father died.

College wasn't for her, so she lived at home with her mom in the Baltimore area. Then came another blow—Gayle's mom died when she was 22.

"It was devastating," Gayle says. "I was a young 22. I wasn't independent." Gayle was bewildered by God. "I didn't think God cared, and I didn't understand Him. I was mad."

Gayle lived a party lifestyle. She had a good job, made money, went out with friends, and eventually, followed a boyfriend to New

York City. "From age 22 until I was 38, I did not talk to God," she recalls. "But I started getting tired."

Seeing nothing but emptiness ahead, Gayle prayed her first prayer in 16 years while walking down Central Park South on her way to work. "I was concerned because I was going to be 40 and I wanted a husband. I didn't want to be alone," she says. "I asked God for a husband. My first prayer was a selfish prayer, but God was waiting for me.

Two months later, Bob York entered her life. After their first date, she knew he was the man God had chosen for her. They married two years later and began enjoying married life. "I had an unusual marriage," says Gayle. "I always say we laughed for 10 years. Most importantly, I had the experience of a husband who loved me more than his own life, and I loved him with all my heart."

Then in 2006, their lives changed abruptly. Almost overnight Bob became deathly ill with pyoderma gangrenosum (PG), a rare autoimmune disorder. After months of daily fevers and pain, treatments and surgeries, doctors finally settled on a medication. But as the illness cleared up, they learned the PG had masked an underlying case of acute myelogenous leukemia.

Although he was weak from fighting off the PG, Bob endured chemotherapy and a bone marrow transplant. But it was too late. He never really recovered. Bob was sent home from the hospital for good on March 13, 2008, and died five days later. "I was praying in the living room, asking God to please take him and not let him suffer any longer," Gayle says. "I said, 'Amen,' and my brother came in to tell me Bob was gone."

Bob's fight was over, but Gayle's biggest battle was about to begin. "I wasn't prepared for the grief," she said. "It was worse than anything I had been through to that point. I felt a lot of bitterness and anger toward God, questioning Him, questioning His purpose and why I should even live. It was a dark place."

One day, God took Gayle to two passages in Psalms. The first was Psalm 88. "He showed me a picture of total devastation," Gayle says. "He was acknowledging my pain, and He acknowledged everything I had seen and experienced." But then God showed Gayle Psalm 71:20-21, which reads: "Though you have made me see troubles, many and bitter, you will restore my life again; from the depths of the earth you will again bring me up. You will increase my honor and comfort me once more."

Those verses were a beacon of hope to Gayle. "You know when the Holy Spirit speaks to you, and I knew this was a message from God." Although she had seen many troubles, the Lord had told her that He would restore her life, increase her honor, and comfort her again.

Gayle visited her brother in Atlanta over Memorial Day weekend, just two months after Bob's death. On a whim, she looked at a house on the market and knew God was bringing her to Atlanta. She sold her home in New Jersey and made the move. But her grief lingered. Although she saw God working in her life, she slipped back into familiar comfort patterns—drinking, partying, and doing whatever she could to numb her pain.

Finally, by fall 2009, she couldn't bear it any longer. She'd heard about GriefShare, a 13-week support group ministry with Scripture-based lessons held at The Church of The Apostles. "I limped in and literally collapsed into GriefShare," Gayle says. "I was like a soldier coming in from battle, broken and worn out."

The first person she met shared the story of losing his wife. Gayle realized at long last there was someone who knew how she felt. "And he gave me hope," she says, "because he looked so happy and content."

The first line of the first page of the GriefShare manual reads, "Grief is maddening." Gayle agrees. "It's the loneliest place on earth, and you feel like you're losing your mind." But through the 13-week course and hearing other people's stories, Gayle began to heal.

Gayle got so much out of the course that she took it a second time, picking up things she'd missed before. By that point, having made friends with others in the group, Gayle knew she'd found a church home at Apostles.

"My grief doesn't own me anymore," she says. "I still miss Bob, and when I cry, it's because of the loss. But I think one day that will change. More than anything, I'm in awe of God that he brought Bob into my life. We had that great life together, and then I was able to take care of him when he was sick. That's what I think of now. I'm thankful and grateful."

***

*Alan Weng*
*Reaching Out through Leading The Way*

Alan used to tell people that he was "made in Taiwan." But now that he's come to know the truth in the Bible, that God sows us in our mother's womb, he says that "*God* made me in Taiwan."

Alan was born in Taiwan and lived there until he was 12, when his father was assigned to work at the Taiwanese Embassy in the US. He went to middle school and high school in the US and then graduated from the University of Maryland in 2004.

But Alan did not have God in his life. He dabbled in the wrong circle of friends after graduation, chasing the fast life—racing motorcycles and partying in nightclubs. But then in 2008, Alan was playing basketball when he took a step back and his Achilles tendon suddenly ripped. He had to have surgery, and afterward, the friends he'd hung out with didn't take the time to see how he was doing. They acted like they didn't care.

Once he had recovered enough to walk, his brother invited him to go to church. That Sunday was August 11, 2008, and that morning he heard a pastor preach about godly courtship and marriage. The message was unlike anything Alan had ever heard from the media or popular culture.

"At that point, God convicted me," Alan says. "I had done everything wrong. I was a sinner."

He was baptized on March 15, 2009. During the next six months, he learned about Jesus and the stories of His life, but he still didn't have a personal relationship with Him. Instead, Alan tried to live by rules. He tried to abide by the Ten Commandments, which he found to be very hard. And living by the Sermon on the Mount he found to be "impossible."

During that time, he felt like he was falling. He couldn't keep up with the rules. He would think of something he had done wrong, and then another, and then another. He was despondent and figured there was no way he could ever "do this Christian thing."

But then one night he turned on the television and found a Leading The Way program, "Know Your Best Friend, Part 2." It was just starting, and there was a flame on the screen and beautiful violin music playing in the background. Then the picture transitioned to the golden cross in our sanctuary. The images and music caught Alan's attention.

On that program, I preached on knowing the Holy Spirit, the third person of the trinity. The words that the Spirit had given me reached out to Alan.

Something changed within him. The Holy Spirit was at work. Weekend after weekend, friends called him, wanting him to ride motorcycles and go to nightclubs, but he had no desire to do that anymore. "The Lord blocked out all those desires, and I just fixed my eyes on watching Leading The Way."

Then twice he "snuck" over to Apostles. He didn't realize he could go to any church he wanted to. Here, he heard testimonies of what God had done in hopeless situations, such as addictions or messy marriages. The stories amazed him. From that time on, Alan started to really know Jesus Christ. Through the actual experiences of others, he saw that God was "truly a perfector, a creator. He could go into any impossible situation and turn it around."

When Alan realized he could attend Apostles, he started attending our Living Waters program. "God brought me to Living Waters," he says, and through that program, he "truly understood how filthy I was." But the people of Apostles reached out to him and were loving and supportive. God worked in Alan's life through the people of Apostles, and he felt God's presence at our church.

Alan had felt lost in the world, but God's love moved him deeply. "I wasn't even alive. I was like a walking zombie, not knowing that he is dead. But He gave me life."

"When you encounter Jesus Christ, nothing can compare to Him because He's so pure and loving." One of Alan's favorite verses is John 15:5: "I am the vine; you are the branches. If you remain in me and I in you, you will bear much fruit; apart from me you can do nothing."

Today, Alan prays that he will continue to bear fruit. That he will decrease and Jesus Christ will increase and fulfill His design for Alan's life.

"I've gone through the fire, but the Lord constantly tells me to look up. He quiets my heart and tells me to look up."

*Chapter Twenty-Seven*

## Blessings

Serving The Church of The Apostles has been a great blessing. It has brought me joy even when it has tested me. We have stood for the truth of the gospel when certain positions were unpopular. And because of those positions, I have been attacked with lies and all sorts of nasty things. When those attacks have come from other Christians, and other pastors, it has hurt. It has not always been easy to accept what others have said about me. At times, things were so bad that we had to install bullet-proof glass in my office (which overlooks the interstate). But that's the price of leadership.

However, I have only felt joy when unbelievers have criticized me. That doesn't mean that I've necessarily *enjoyed* the criticism. I don't desire it. But if I'm doing my job, I should expect Satan to attack me. If I go a while without his attack, I begin to wonder if I'm traveling in the same direction as him.

More than ever, I understand what it means when Jesus says, "Blessed are you when people insult you, persecute you and falsely say all kinds of evil against you because of me." When people say terrible things about me, I know that I'm in Christ and not compromising. I'm trying to please the Lord and not people. When I know I am abiding in the Lord, I am joyful.

Fortunately, for twenty-five years, the people of Apostles have blessed me by standing with me when I've been criticized.

\*\*\*

Starting a church is a lot like raising a child. You have a baby. You feed her, change her, take care of her. You stay up at night when she's sick. You agonize when she falls after taking her first steps, and later, when she's learning to ride a bike. She grows older, goes through adolescence, and you support her and sometimes argue with her. Sometimes your shared experiences are beautiful, and other times they're painful. But as she becomes an adult, the painful stuff fades into the background, because now you have an adult who is now your friend, someone who is your partner in life.

Apostles is a church that I birthed through God's grace and the help of others. Many of our experiences were beautiful and a few were painful. But after 25 years, the pain has faded. We are partners in ministry, and I am filled with joy when I see how mature in Christ our church has become.

Now I want to challenge us to not rest in our maturity, but to plant the word of God in more places. That's why recently we trained 1,500 adults from our church to share Christ with others. Everyone does not have the gift of evangelism, but we all have the ability to witness, to give an account of our faith to others. We might witness in a different style depending on our unique gifts. But we can all give our testimony nonetheless.

That is now part of everyone's responsibility at Apostles—to share the gospel. Several years ago, we started our transition from being a "cruise ship" to becoming an "aircraft carrier." A cruise ship is a place that's all about having fellowship and eating and being happy together. And that's great. But as an aircraft carrier, we want to send our membership out into the field. Apostles can be a place for people to come back to and get refueled, but eventually, they will head back out into the field again.

We train our members to go out and be soul winners—to live an apostle's life, to make new disciples just as Jesus instructed us. It doesn't matter if those new believers end up worshipping at Apostles. Our concern is not bringing people into the pews; our concern is bringing people into the Kingdom of God.

In another twenty-five years, my hope is that we will have multiplied ourselves many times over. That our passion will have grown even stronger. That through personal evangelism, and our Leading The Way and THE KINGDOM SAT programs, we will have served God well.

\*\*\*

In 2009, Leading The Way organized an enormous evangelical outreach in Alexandria, Egypt. It was held on the Catholic cathedral grounds and involved 105 local churches from numerous denominations. We had 27 buses bringing people in from all over the area.

During the outreach, the believers in Alexandria held a prayer meeting that lasted all night. It was a powerful night, and I could tell God was doing some great things. Once, after I finished preaching, I exited the stage and went to a side area with many of the other pastors. There, I spotted an older gentleman who seemed familiar. When he introduced himself to me I was stunned.

"I'm Wesley," he said.

"Wesley!"

I was so excited to see him. Wesley was a friend of my older brothers. But most importantly, he was the son of Pastor Girgis, who all those years ago had heard from God and had convinced my parents not to abort me.

Wesley, who was now 78 years old, was there with his sister. I said to both of them, "If it wasn't for the faithfulness of your father, I wouldn't be here!"

They smiled, and Wesley said, "We know. We know the story."

It was such a blessing to visit with Pastor Girgis's children and say that to them. And it was a reminder of how much God had honored Pastor Girgis's obedience.

If I could talk to Pastor Girgis today, I would tell him, "Thank you for listening to God. Thank you for your courage, for speaking the truth." He knew that something bad could have happened to my mother and he would live with the consequences for the rest of his life. He could have doubted God's voice. He could have felt it was none of his business and not said anything. Instead he trusted and obeyed.

***

Because of Pastor Girgis's trustful obedience, I have led a blessed life. And for twenty-five years of that life, I have been blessed by The Church of The Apostles. I have enjoyed the privilege of not only helping to start a church and watching it grow, but of watching God work through it in many wonderful ways.

How has Apostles blessed me?

The opportunity to lead our church in vibrant and meaningful worship—filled with singing, prayer, and teaching—has blessed me.

The opportunity to witness the energetic growth of our children's ministry and Student to Student ministry—which reach, equip, and mobilize students to do the work of God—has blessed me.

The sharing of biblical knowledge through our abundant classes and groups for men, women, young families, and young adults; and the prayers and lively discussions of our weekly small groups—those have blessed me.

An attentive and loving congregation—that cares for people dealing with divorce, grief, addictions, and financial problems, and that supports caregivers, peacemakers, military personnel, the homebound, and children with special needs—has blessed me.

I have been blessed because intercessory prayer is a way of life at Apostles.

I have been blessed because we have been privileged to take the Gospel of Jesus Christ to our community and to 190 countries and to the ends of the earth.

Most of all, the trust and obedience of The Church of The Apostles has blessed me. That has been our single greatest mission for 25 years. God has guided us, and we have done our best to follow. Through trustful obedience, Apostles has helped to enlarge the Kingdom of God and enrich the lives of His followers.

Through His mercy, we will do the same with even more passion and energy for the next 25 years—and beyond.

To God be ALL the glory.